Praise for Edwin Martin's

BREAKTHROUGH

Ed Martin's participant-observer account of how and why the Individuals with Disabilities Education Act (IDEA) became the most important special education law of the land is as rich in detail as it is engaging. Although much of the narrative refers to people and events of the 1960s and 1970s, the book is a powerful and inspirational reminder to policymakers, advocates, and practitioners in the present why special education is a necessary and noble profession.

Douglas Fuchs
Professor and Nicholas Hobbs Chair
of Special Education and Human Development
Vanderbilt University

Edwin Martin, a pivotal force behind the development of federal policy in special education, combines facts, humor and sensitivity with a plethora of amazing stories about the politics, personalities and behind-the-scenes maneuvering involved. A fascinating read and an important contribution to the field of education!

Sally C. Grimes, Ed. M.
Founding Director
The Grimes Reading Institute

Breakthrough is a wonderfully wise and readable perspective on the meaning of special education, the creation of federal legislation, and the personal contributions of the author and others in enactment of the law now known as the Individuals with Disabilities Education Act. It is a must read for anyone who cares about policies affecting the education of students with disabilities.

James Kauffman.
Professor Emeritus of Education
University of Virginia

Bardolf & Company

BREAKTHROUGH
Federal Special Education Legislation 1965-1981

ISBN 978-0-9836184-9-2

Published by Bardolf & Company
5430 Colewood Pl.
Sarasota, FL 34232
941-232-0113
www.bardolfandcompany.com

Cover design and layout by Shaw Creative
www.shawcreativegroup.com

DEDICATION

To Peggy, who has encouraged me
for years to write this book.

And to my sons, Scott and Bruce,
and grandchildren Alec and Gwen,
a loving community
that shares common values
with Peggy and with me.

BREAKTHROUGH

Federal Special Education Legislation 1965–1981

Edwin W. Martin

Bardolf & Company
Sarasota, Florida

CONTENTS

ACKNOWLEDGMENTS

There are numerous people I feel grateful to. Many are named on these pages and recognized for the work to help bring equal educational opportunity to children with disabilities. Others have helped me and encouraged me to tell this story.

Don Deshler gave me above and beyond support in developing this book. Sally Grimes and Joan Sedita, friends from my Harvard seminar, have supported my work and played significant roles in developing public policy and new programming for reading improvement. Dan Hallahan and Jim Kauffman, colleagues at the University of Virginia, have offered encouragement, support and models in their publications. Doug and Lynn Fuchs, long-time colleagues and friends in the learning disability struggles, helped me with the fundamentals of Response to Intervention.

A special thank you to my editor, Chris Angermann, whose editorial skills were so obvious that I lost any sense of stubborn dedication to my words. Readers owe Chris thanks as well, as he has made this a much more readable book.

And finally, thanks to you, my readers, for being interested in this story about a landmark change in American educational policy.

INTRODUCTION

On a visit to China in 1988, I saw a cardboard figure of a warrior outside the Ming Tombs near Beijing. The man was fighting a tiger, a broken stick near his side. There was a cutout where a visitor could put his or her head on the body and assume the identity of the warrior for a photograph.

At the time, I was in China as a guest speaker for the first international conference on special education hosted by that giant nation. My task, an unenviable one perhaps, was to make the final remarks; the organizers wanted me to pull the conference together—after the potpourri of ideas and perceptions from specialists of different nations. I didn't feel up to the challenge. I knew that I could not manage to encapsulate dozens of papers, or even highlight the many subjects addressed.

As I looked at the cardboard figure I recognized it must be a myth, similar to others—Beowulf and Grendel, David and Goliath—in which man struggles to overcome a stronger external force.

That night I had the pleasure of meeting novelist Bette Bao Lord and her husband, Winston Lord, who was then Ambassador of the United States to China. I asked Mrs. Lord about the man and the tiger and she immediately replied it was Wu Song, the hero of the epic "Water Margin," and the next day she kindly sent me a short synopsis of the myth.

Wu Song had many strengths, but was most famous for his ability to slay tigers. One day during his travels he passed a small inn at the foot of the Jin Yang Mountains. A sign in the window read,

"Three bowls and you will never make it across." Curious, he asked and discovered that the mountains were notorious for the fierce tigers that roamed there. A traveler who drank too much wine and lay down to sleep would not survive.

Wu Song, in the manner of mythic heroes, was not deterred. He called for nine bowls of wine. (Nine is a magic number in China and the palaces of emperors displayed decorations in units of nine.) He downed the nine bowls and set off for the mountains.

Soon, he began to feel sleepy, but when he lay down to rest a tiger came along and attacked him. They battled long and hard and Wu Song's only weapon, a club, split in half in the fury of the fight. Undaunted, the warrior grabbed a stone from the ground and overcame the tiger.

As have many other mythical figures, Wu Song demonstrated that individuals can accomplish what common wisdom warns is impossible.

I realized the story gave me a universal theme that I could use to tie together the various strands of the special education conference. Myths, although stories, point the way to a truth. A detail like Wu Song's club splitting has meaning for all of us. It suggests that things don't always work as planned and we must be prepared to improvise a new solution. I told the conferees, "You are Wu Song. I am Wu Song." The audience greeted that concept warmly, as it communicated across cultures.[1]

***

Discrimination toward people with disabilities is centuries old and crosses cultures. People who suffer from a disability have been

---

1 Later, Deborah Deutsch Smith and Ruth Luckasson used the story as I told it as a preface to their book, "Introduction to Special Education: Teaching in an Age of Challenge," Allyn & Bacon (1992).

ignored, rejected, isolated and sometimes exterminated. In the United States they have been excluded from societal activities, institutionalized, and until relatively recently, treated as second-class citizens.

In the 1960s, under Presidents Kennedy and Johnson, the federal government began to study the participation of people with disabilities in society and schools and build a public policy designed to overturn past injustices and provide "equal opportunity." The federal role came about because parents petitioned the national government on behalf of their children with disabilities after they felt the responses by officials at local and state governmental levels were not adequate.

I had the good fortune to be an "inside player" in bringing about significant changes in national public policy, working from 1965 to 1981 for the Congress and for the Executive Branch, and directing the federal special education program under four Presidents, Johnson, Nixon, Ford and Carter. My purpose in recalling these events is not only to share my perceptions of this history, its key issues and players, but also to suggest lessons that have been learned which have relevance now and in the future.

***

We all are Wu Song. We must face the tigers in our own lives.

In our work with children and adults with disabilities, we face tigers. Some of the tigers may be society's fear and rejection of people with disabilities. Some may be our own limitations. We must use imagination and improvisation to overcome these tigers.

In special education we seek to end centuries of fear, rejection and exclusion. We seek to educate children with significant learning problems. We seek what "common wisdom warned was impossible."

Our work has shown that it is possible to reach our goal, perhaps not all at once, but gradually we can overcome the tiger.

PART ONE

Early Beginnings

This book follows the development of federal legislation to initiate, expand and improve education for children with disabilities over a period of more than 15 years, starting in 1965. In those days, they were generally referred to as "the handicapped." I became engaged in that process early on while working for four months as an "expert" in the U.S. Office of Education's Division of Handicapped Children and Youth. My work there as a professional interested in speech and hearing disorders brought me in contact with a few key people with similar interests in the Congressional staff and the Department of Health, Education and Welfare. That, in turn, led me to be offered a position, in 1966, as director of a House of Representatives subcommittee studying special education needs in the United States.

CHAPTER 1

Why Federal Law Was Necessary

In 1966, Representative Hugh L. Carey (Democrat, NY), was named chairman of a newly created ad hoc Subcommittee on the Handicapped. The "ad hoc" signified its temporary nature. Unlike a permanent or "standing" subcommittee, it would have to be reappointed by the chairman of the parent committee, Education and Labor, in every subsequent Congress.

Carey, a relative newcomer to Washington and a Democrat, represented a Republican-leaning district in Brooklyn. He had been a friend of John F. Kennedy, and was first elected when he ran with him in 1960. He was not a "knee jerk liberal" by any means, but a moderate with fiscal common sense, (as later demonstrated by his success as New York's Governor, when he brought New York City back from financial ruin). He had to have powerful backing to gain a subcommittee chairmanship, even an "ad hoc" one, as his seniority did not entitle him to one of the six standing subcommittees.

He had good relations with the chairman of the Education and Labor Committee, the controversial Congressman from Harlem, Adam Clayton Powell (Democrat, NY), who, as a chairman, could create ad hoc subcommittees. Carey had worked closely with Powell to frame and pass the landmark Elementary and Secondary Education Act of 1965 (ESEA). ESEA began the modern era of federal aid to the schools after years of bitter controversy involving issues such as the constitutionality of federal education aid, funding for segregated schools and funding for private, particularly Roman Catholic, schools. Carey was a key player in shaping the provisions that allowed certain kinds of funding to flow to children enrolled in parochial schools.

Carey's other powerful ally was Representative John Fogarty (Democrat, RI) who chaired the Appropriations Subcommittee for Health, Education, Welfare and Labor. Committees like Education and Labor, Defense, and Agriculture write the laws that spell out the terms of federal programs, for example, aid to disadvantaged children. They are called "authorizing" committees. But it is the Appropriations Committee which has the power to create funding for those programs. Without the necessary dollars, most federal programs were meaningless. So powerful were the subcommittee chairmen of the Appropriations Committee that they were often called "The College of Cardinals" (a good number were also Irish-Americans).[2]

Chairman Fogarty was a compassionate man. In 1957 he had provided funding for research into the education of children with mental retardation, after being urged to do so at a social gathering by the parent of a child with that disability. He also had been a prime mover in creating the National Institute of Health (NIH), along with Senator Lister Hill (Democrat, AL), chairman of the Senate HEW-Labor Appropriations Subcommittee. Overruling Presidents, Republican or Democratic, Fogarty and Hill each year

---

2 Note: The culture of the House of Representatives included referring to members by title of Mr., Miss or Mrs. In discussion or debate on the floor of the House, members refer to other members as "The gentleman from New York" or "The gentle-lady from Oregon." If a Congressman or Congresswoman, (Senators are Senators, not ever addressed as Congressman or woman) were chairman of a committee or subcommittee the proper form of address was, "Mr. Chairman," or, in the third person, "Chairman So and so." The usage for women was not always consistent in the 60s or 70s so that one might hear "Madame Chairman" and less frequently, if ever, "Chairwoman" or "Chairlady." To fail to address someone deserving the title as "Chairman" was a serious faux pas.

provided NIH with more funds than proposed in the President's budget. Today, buildings on the NIH campus are named for each.

Should Chairman Carey be able to secure Congressional passage of legislation authorizing the assistance of the education of children with disabilities, Chairman Fogarty could make the program a reality by having his subcommittee appropriate the necessary funds. Fogarty's ability to support legislation with funding would have natural appeal for Chairman Powell, who was committed to improving education for poor and minority children, and so Fogarty's interest in Carey's subcommittee to study education for children with disabilities offered potential benefits for Powell's education agenda.

In the Senate, Chairman Hill had demonstrated interest in disability issues, and so the time seemed ripe for an examination of the need for new legislation. In addition to the HEW-Labor Appropriations subcommittee, Hill also chaired the Labor and Public Welfare authorization committee, which wrote the legislation in those areas and in education. It gave him enormous and unrivaled power in these matters.

How Congressional Hearings Work

Organizing a Congressional hearing is not a random activity, announcing the subject and taking volunteers who wish to speak. Instead, most hearings are carefully planned by the staff members at the direction of their "principals" and designed with witnesses selected to present a point of view that the chairman or committee members already support or consider a potential interest. When an issue is controversial, with the political parties having differing views, the members of the minority party often protest that the chairman and the majority staff don't grant them sufficient time to present their witnesses, although they always have some opportunity to do so.

I arrived in Washington in the spring of 1966, a 34-year-old Associate Professor of Speech Pathology at the University of Alabama, with no background in the legislative process. I had spent four months, in 1965, as an "expert," for the U.S. Office of Education's programs involving special education. That experience turned out to have great value, since it allowed me to understand the problems and strengths of the federal grant programs from the point of view of the people working in them, and also to recognize the perceptions of grantees from the nation's special education community. Those perceptions became a central focus of the hearings.

The Alabama tie also turned out to be relevant to my getting involved with Carey's committee through my work on programs for deaf children with Patria Winalski, then the Executive Secretary of the National Advisory Committee on the Deaf, housed in the Department of Health, Education and Welfare (HEW). During my 1965 stay in Washington, I met Winalski and her friend John (Jack) Forsythe, the general counsel for Senator Hill's Committee on Labor and Public Welfare, which included jurisdiction for health and education legislation among its various charges. To have legislation passed, i.e., by Carey, the corresponding authority in the Senate would be necessary. The general counsel of a committee has enormous power in representing the chair, often more power than other members, although it must be exercised very carefully to preserve the chairman's approval. Winalski told me that Representative Edith Green (Democrat, OR) sarcastically called Jack "Senator Forsythe" when she was frustrated by his actions.[3]

While in Alabama, I had worked with my colleague Tom Giolas as co-director of the Speech and Hearing Clinic to start a joint program

---

3 Actually, it was Charlie Lee, education staff specialist for Senator Wayne Morse, who Mrs. Green called "Senator." Morse was a converted Republican who became the chairman of the Senate Education Committee and Green was probably bitter about Morse occupying that Senate seat and about Charlie's power and influence. I found out that Green's remark was actually about Charles "Charlie" Lee, the chief education staff specialist for Senator Wayne Morse (Democrat, OR), not Jack Forsythe, reflecting the rivalry between fellow Oregonians. Professor Gareth Davies of Oxford University is a leading scholar in American educational policy and in his research he discovered the accurate account from an interview with Charlie Lee and passed it on to me. We had shared notes about our respective research projects. Pat Winalski Forsythe sometimes did not let accuracy stand in the way of a good story.

with Jasper Harvey, head of the Special Education Department. For the first time in Alabama, teachers of the deaf were trained at the university level. Winalski, the mother of a child who was deaf, was happy to find an ally and realized that my ties with Alabama might help gain Senator Hill's support for new programs to assist persons who were deaf. Her friend, later husband, Jack, called me and arranged to introduce me to Hugh Carey when he was organizing his subcommittee. My professional background, along with my being a native New Yorker and, most importantly, my potential help in securing Chairman Hill's support for legislation in the Senate, probably all led Carey to offer me the job of staff director of the subcommittee.

Carey estimated the subcommittee's work would last from May through the summer, unless we developed support for legislation that could extend the subcommittee's life. My job was to organize the hearings, create a comprehensive record of inquiry, and hopefully, help design a new federal law. The title of "director" sounded impressive even though the entire staff I was to direct consisted of an administrative assistant, Loretta Bowen, a part-time secretary, Rosemary King[4], and one "no show" appointed by the minority party; but I soon realized that my position, like the general counsel mentioned before, has considerable power. In fact, much of the work of Congress is done by staff members, generally with a great deal of independence. Even as a neophyte I found that I exercised considerable independence in affecting legislation and, therefore, national policy.

Carey knew that the Council for Exceptional Children (CEC) had an agenda for federal legislation and he suggested I meet with its executive director, William Geer. CEC was and is the leading organization of teachers and higher education professionals interested in teaching children with disabilities (and gifted and talented children). I began planning

4 Rosemary was married to Larry L. King, then known primarily as a young man who came to Washington to work for a liberal Texas Congressman (yes, there was such a thing). King had written for the *Texas Monthly* and was part of a group of bright, literate, up and coming authors. I had enjoyed his collection of stories, "My Hero LBJ and Other SOBs." He later wrote the book for the musical "The Best Little Whorehouse in Texas."

the hearings with his input. Geer was a veteran at CEC and in Washington, and he had been involved in various earlier efforts, some successful and some unsuccessful, to build federal legislation. He was happy to have a disability specialist as staff director—even if I was a speech pathologist, coming from a profession that generally does not see itself as part of special education, nor is seen as such by special educators—and we quickly became friends and allies. I admired his knowledge, calm demeanor and his political instincts and began planning the hearings with his input.

I also began to contact other organizations interested in disability—specialty groups interested in mental retardation, mental health, blindness, deafness, the newly emerging area of learning disabilities, cerebral palsy and, of course, speech and hearing disorders. Many of these groups were organized by parents. I quickly came to admire their knowledge and untiring advocacy. I realized that parents had provided the energy and will to create special education programs wherever they occurred. They had petitioned school administrators, school board members, state officials, state legislators and, increasingly, federal legislators and administrators. It became apparent to me that there would be little, if any, special education if the parents had not created it, directly or through political persuasion. CEC, as an organization of professionals, was an effective ally and always worked on behalf of children, not as an advocate for teachers' interests as opposed to their charges.

The lesson that parents provided the energy and "emotional power" behind legislative efforts can be generalized. Persons interested in healthcare, veteran's benefits, the environment, etc. need to present their case by including input from a significant number of people directly involved, not just scientists and program administrators.

Background to Hearings of Carey Subcommittee

It is traditional for the "Administration" to lead off a series of hearings by presenting a statement from the ranking official in the Executive

Branch with responsibility for the content area of the hearings. In this case that official would have been Harold Howe II, the U.S. Commissioner of Education. But when the hearings began, Howe did not appear, sending instead his Deputy, Graham Sullivan. Carey was offended, believing the substitution indicated the Commissioner and perhaps the Administration were not taking his ad hoc subcommittee seriously.

There were several reasons why that might have been the case. Although the Johnson Administration sponsored and secured approval for education legislation at a rate not seen previously or since that time, disability was not on its priority list. Johnson's focus was on improving the educational system for people who were economically disadvantaged. He felt that the primary route for overcoming the effects of racism and segregation, as well as the comparable problems of poor, white persons, would be through education. Programs for preschool children and children in low-income neighborhoods; programs to provide technical and vocational education and jobs; and programs to make higher education accessible to all—these were the backbone of Johnson's plan to end or reduce poverty. It was not that there was any negative attitude toward disability, it was just "invisible"—something true in society in general at that time.

***

Years later, while I was teaching at the Harvard Graduate School of Education, I had the privilege of getting to know Francis Keppel, a brilliant and practical man who served as Commissioner of Education under President Kennedy and continued through the beginning of the Johnson Administration. "Frank" Keppel told me that President Johnson realized the price he would pay politically for passing the Civil Rights Act, the Voting Rights Act and various education and social programs. He told the top officials as he came into office that he had about 18 months before his positive ratings and political support, particularly in the South, would disappear. He challenged them to get his major education programs, The Elementary and Secondary Education Act of 1965, The Higher Education Act of 1965 and similar legislation, passed before his political capital ran out. It was the most ambitious education agenda in the nation's history.

The legislation was passed and, as predicted, the capital dwindled. In retrospect, Johnson's commitment to Civil Rights is even more impressive, considering his awareness of what it would cost him and the Democratic Party. President Nixon organized his successful 1968 campaign around the "Southern Strategy," which continues to dominate the Republican Party today.

I had a small but powerful demonstration of Johnson's deep feelings about education when I was one of a group invited to the White House for a bill signing and to hear the President's remarks on education. It was not the best place to deliver a speech. As the President stood in the Rose Garden, he had to stop each time a jet flew down the Potomac River on its way to National Airport. After repeated interruptions, he shrugged, smiled and said, "This really is a lousy place to live. It's so noisy with these planes, and when I'm up in the family quarters on the top floor trying to take a nap, there are thousands of tourists tromping through the public rooms just below my bedroom, or Ladybird is standing out on the balcony talking with Laurance Rockefeller about some goddamn daffodils."

Still, the speech was memorable. Johnson began and then folded the prepared papers and put them in his jacket pocket, speaking extemporaneously. He told of his mother's deep commitment to education and his own early days as a teacher in a one-room school in San Marcos, Texas. His feelings were so obviously real that the audience was spellbound. I told my wife that night that if the President, who so often seemed wooden and uninvolved in his public speeches, could only communicate the way he did that day, people would feel much more positively about him.

***

Another reason why the Commissioner of Education might have decided not to appear before the Carey subcommittee is that he believed it was established in the summer before the November 1966 election mostly to get some visibility for its chairman, something to campaign on back in Brooklyn. In any event, Howe's decision not to appear created a negative attitude toward the Office of Education in the subcommittee, which was quickly amplified by the way the Office reorganized certain programs.

Bill Geer had told me that CEC hoped to see Carey introduce legislation to provide funds directly to the states for supporting special education. They also wanted to have a bureau, the highest-level subunit of the office, for administration of programs for the disabled. A Division of Handicapped Children and Youth, (one level below a bureau), had been established just before President Kennedy's assassination. Dr. Samuel Kirk, arguably the leading special educator in the nation had agreed, at the President's request, to take a six-month leave of absence from the University of Illinois to start the agency. Morale was high in the special education field.

Unfortunately, in 1965, the division was caught up in a major reorganization necessitated by all the new education legislation which had vast grant programs to administer. As a result, the existing small federal special education authorities, i.e., a program of grants to colleges and universities to support training of teachers; a very small research and demonstration program; and a program which loaned captioned (subtitled) films to organizations of deaf persons were dispersed to other larger bureaus, and the Division of Handicapped Children and Youth was abolished.

Adding insult to injury, the most important program—which provided scholarships and support grants to colleges and universities for the training of educators—was subsumed by a division that had the training of regular educators as its focus. Its leaders hoped to use the funding for special education to create programs for "regular" educators to have special education in their regular training. The goal was to end special education, per se. Although some view a similar concept positively today, it was a very unpopular concept then. Special education advocates did not necessarily reject efforts to "mainstream" children with disabilities into regular education, but because the Office of Education policies were not clearly spelled out, did not grow out of any careful study of issues and had not involved special educators in the planning, they felt considerable anxiety and resentment. One assumption of the new program director appeared to be that special educators would not be needed to help children in regular programs.

Parents Describe the Problems their Children Faced

As I met with parent group representatives in preparation for the hearings I was stunned by the lack of services they reported. The schools routinely turned their children away. Those with disabilities such as deafness or blindness were often required to travel far from home to a state-operated residential school if they wished to receive any special education.

In local school programs, children were frequently subjected to substandard services in poor facilities. Parents reported classes in basements, janitor's rooms, condemned buildings and similar sites. Children were often placed in classes inappropriate for their needs, for example, it was not uncommon to find students with cerebral palsy, no matter what their intelligence level, placed in classes for children with mental retardation.

Even where programs were offered, they frequently were not staffed by appropriately trained teachers, and instructors generally had to create their own curricula and materials. Supplies were limited or non-existent. Parents sometimes organized their own programs outside of school. The National Association for Retarded Citizens, (now The Arc), the United Cerebral Palsy Association, the Easter Seal program and many other local and state groups organized classes and schools, often staffing them with parents.

As a speech pathologist working in Alabama in the 1950s and 60s, I was familiar with the lack of services for children with speech and hearing disorders in that rural state, which was regarded as having one of the nation's poorest educational systems. I had no idea, however, that not a single state even pretended to educate all of its children with disabilities. Even states that had "Mandatory Laws," i.e., laws requiring the local districts to offer special education, did not enforce them. The laws themselves generally had loopholes, such as allowing the local school officials to decide when a child could not "benefit" from instruction, or when instruction for a given child might not be "feasible."

As the hearings moved forward and members of the subcommittee heard this type of testimony, they also were shocked. Most had very little knowledge of disability issues. Carey was somewhat more aware, having visited special education programs and schools in his district. He also had co-sponsored with John Fogarty a 1965 Act, "The National Technical Institute for the Deaf," which created the first post-secondary program designed to provide vocational and technical education. Gallaudet University in Washington, D.C. was the only college in the world designed for persons who were deaf, but it offered only a liberal arts program.

Also in 1965, Carey had introduced an amendment, (PL 89-313), to Title I of the Elementary and Secondary Education Act, (ESEA), which provided grants to each state for every child enrolled in a "state-operated" or "state-supported" school for disabled children. In the northeast and in New York, there were a number of such schools, including those sponsored by the Roman Catholic Church. Because the children in all of these schools received state support, this amendment to the general purposes of the Title—serving disadvantaged children—created a kind of precedent for federal aid to children in parochial schools. This program was undoubtedly suggested by Pat Winalski, as schools for the deaf were primary beneficiaries. Jack Forsythe securing the support of Chairman Hill essentially guaranteed the backing of other Senators. As a prime advocate for federal aid being used to benefit children in parochial schools, Carey saw the disability provision as creating a precedent for wider assistance. (Such aid eventually was allowed under Supreme Court rulings.)

Despite his familiarity with disability issues, Carey was astounded when I told him that the legislation he was considering to support new special education programs would have to serve millions of children. His view of disability was that it concerned only a limited number of children with deafness, blindness or mental retardation, such as those in state schools. Such a population, perhaps one hundred thousand, would be a much more financially feasible target group.

Office of Education Testimony

In their statements, which opened the hearings, Deputy Commissioner of Education Graham Sullivan and Deputy Assistant Secretary of HEW Phillip Des Marais gave further perspective on the problems facing children with disabilities. The government officials had no idea how many children with education-related disabilities there might be in the nation. They had neither a program for counting nor a method of inquiry. (The states did not count either, although some kept track of the numbers reported by local schools to receive state aid. In general, states did not *want* to inquire about those unserved.)

Title I of ESEA was a giant program for its time, with more than one million children receiving benefits from a one billion dollar annual grant to the school districts. (As Senator Everett Dirkson (Republican, IL) famously said, "A billion here, a billion there…first thing you know you are talking about real money.")

Poor children with disabilities were eligible for the act's "compensatory education" programs, such as improving reading performance. The Office of Education had no idea if any children with disabilities were participating. Again, they were not counting. In subsequent years it became known that administrators of Title I discouraged support for programs for children with disabilities, as they observed them competing for limited funds with non-disabled, poor children. Interestingly, even many Head Start program supporters held a similar view. They somehow considered preschoolers with disabilities as less deserving of assistance than their non-disabled peers. We were able to address that problem directly in later years.

The Office of Education officials had no specific plan to benefit children with disabilities in local schools. They did mention their support for the existing grant programs for training teachers and for research. This absence of federal initiative, coupled with the painful testimony of parents that followed, created a premise for a new federal program which would provide funds to local districts in order to offer additional special education services to children. The challenge would be to secure support from the Administration's Office of Management and Budget, (then called Bureau of the Budget). It had to approve any program which was to become part of the "President's Budget" and be presented to the Congress as a presidential recommendation for action.

Testimony by the Council for Exceptional Children opened the public phase of the hearings after the government witnesses. CEC was represented by its then president, Ernest Willenberg, a school administrator from Los Angeles, and Executive Secretary Bill Geer. As is usual in such testimony, Willenberg, as president and representing an actual district, gave the statement which Geer, the Washington-based professional, had prepared. He outlined the needs of children, emphasizing the lack of programs and the insufficient numbers of teachers, and advocated a three-part solution, which mirrored the conversations I had had with Bill Geer. First, he recommended a federal program of grants to the states, and through them, the local districts; second, a Bureau of Education for the Handicapped within the Office of Education; and third, a national advisory committee which would monitor the educational needs of children with disabilities and report annually to the Commissioner of Education, and through him to the Congress and the public.

Following the testimony of the parents and various professional groups, the subcommittee heard from the Office of Education's new training program director, Dr. Donald Bigelow. When I prepared the schedule for the hearings, I had no idea that his testimony would turn into a hostile confrontation about misusing funds appropriated for disability programs, but as Bigelow spoke of his plans to use the money to promote "mainstreaming," the atmosphere turned frosty. Carey replied that his concern was that children with disabilities might "drown in that mainstream." This concern for how the federal "handicapped" funds would be spent set the stage for Congressional support of a new Bureau of Education for the Handicapped over the opposition of the Office of Education and its parent agency, HEW.

I was delighted by the outcome. I felt the negative energy generated by the hearing could drive the legislation concerning a bureau forward when it might have had hard going in a different climate. I hoped to capitalize on the "good guys vs. bad guys" emotion. Congress frequently gets motivated by clashes with the Executive Branch, even when the President belongs to the same party as the majority. If the disagreement is serious enough, Congress usually prevails since it controls the power of the purse.

The record presented to the subcommittee clearly indicated a great need for special education services and, unfortunately, an absence of federal government initiatives. Further, the reorganization activities and Bigelow's proposed program changes were seen as harming existing efforts rather than strengthening them. Add to this the failure of the Commissioner of Education to appear and the testimony of Bigelow that irritated the subcommittee's chairman and members, and the climate was set for the Congress to take independent action and not wait for an Administration initiative.

CHAPTER 2

The Carey Bill

Even while the subcommittee continued to meet, conducting a visit to the Maryland School for the Deaf and holding further hearings in New York City involving a number of prominent special educators, Chairman Carey directed me to begin drafting a bill. He proposed following the model of the Elementary and Secondary Education Act (ESEA), which contained a number of provisions or "titles." In the Carey Bill, the first title would be a grant program to the states. The second would support library and instructional materials. The third would encourage innovative projects proposed by local districts and non-profit agencies. The fourth would aid research—I suggested adding personnel training as well—and the fifth would provide grants to state education agencies to expand their staffs so they could administer special education programs and the funding under the proposed act.

Carey had in mind a funding formula, similar to his amendment to Title I of ESEA on behalf of children in state schools. That formula offered a federal share for each child based on either the average per-pupil expenditure in that state, or the national average per-pupil expenditure, whichever was greater. ESEA proposed a 10% share of the average per-pupil expenditure the first year, and an additional 10% each following year until a maximum of 40% had been reached. This blueprint for the program would represent an "authorization." Should the Appropriations Committee decide on a lesser sum—as it usually did—the act would have partially fulfilled the formula.

The problem with the proposed formula was Carey's assumption about the number of children with disabilities in the population. As mentioned earlier, it was considerably lower than reality—my estimate at the time was approximately five million, based on the sketchy information available. But even if only one million children required special education, and received just $100 per child, a paltry sum, the program would have cost $100 million—a large amount, indeed, for an "invisible" problem. A 10% share of average per-student expenditure, based on an estimate that costs for a child with a disability would be twice that of a non-disabled child, would have approached $500 million. It simply was not feasible in 1966 to propose such a program to the President, his Bureau of the Budget, and ultimately the Congress.

Carey instructed me to solve the problem. I decided to work with George Skinner, the legislative counsel to the Education and Labor committee, who had been a key player in drafting all the new major education programs. He understood the impossibility of a per-child-based formula, and suggested another model in which legislation would authorize a given amount of money, which could increase each year as the committee desired, (recognizing that the actual sum would depend on the Appropriations Committee's action). Each state would get a share proportional to its population. If state A had 5% of the nation's children of school age (not children with disabilities—an unknown), then it would get 5% of the appropriated funds.

The chairman did not like this solution—he rightly recognized that it was less powerful than a per-child sum. With his approach one could actually count the children in a local program and figure out how much a district would get if Congress appropriated the full allowance. In the proposal Skinner and I submitted, a certain sum would go to the state capital, but it would be divided at the own discretion of the state education office, with the result that local administrators would have less ability to lobby Congress with estimates of exactly how much their schools would receive. Eventually Carey accepted our model and took care to enlist his friend

Speaker John McCormack's assistance in giving the bill a favored number when it was introduced. Carey chose H.R. 14, the number of people in his family at the time, his wife, himself and 12 children. The bill's title was "The Handicapped Children's Education Assistance Act." (Legislation is a "bill" until it is passed by Congress and signed by the President when it becomes an act and is assigned a "Public Law" number.)

Carey invited me to join him on a trip to the White House to talk with one of President Johnson's top education assistants, Douglass Cater. I still have a vivid memory of that first visit to the White House. We entered the gates on Pennsylvania Avenue between the Executive Office Building and the West Wing and aided by Marine guards and Secret Service agents, found our way to Cater's office. I was somewhat awestruck as we walked through the West Wing, up the marble staircase, and into the offices where Cater was located, near the seat of power, the Oval Office. In Washington there is a saying, "Never underestimate proximity."

The message we received was mildly encouraging, but not for the year 1966. It was already early summer, and the President's budget had been in place since January. The best we could look forward to was a "blessing" for the next year's budget. No particular dollar sum was agreed to. I went back to work thinking we could attempt to get Congress to act, and it is doubtful that the President would veto it. However, getting funds from the Appropriations Committees for an act not in the President's budget would be a much higher hurdle.

Rookie Mistakes

At the time, Robert Kennedy was the "Junior" Senator from New York, (the longest serving Senator from a state is the "Senior Senator"). He announced that he would hold hearings on disability issues under the auspices of the Government Operations Committee on which he served. Carey's reaction was difficult for me to discern. I knew he had friendly relations with the Senator, as he had had with the late President John F. Kennedy, but I suspected he also feared the hearings might impinge on his plans. He never really told me what he thought, but "ownership" of a bill is highly prized, and if Kennedy should decide to sponsor legislation, his greater public profile would submerge Carey's. Government Operations, however, did not have legislative jurisdiction for writing authorizing bills in the area of education for children with disabilities. In the Senate, that was the domain of Chairman Hill's Committee on Labor and Public Welfare and its Education Subcommittee, then chaired by Senator Wayne Morse.

Kennedy could conceivably argue he was reviewing the operation of already existing federal programs, but it seemed likely that he wanted to demonstrate an interest in the disability area and make a public statement, perhaps sponsoring a bill even if only the Education Committee could pursue the legislation. Certainly, his family had made a major commitment to programming for persons with disabilities. President Kennedy had signed the first Community Mental Retardation Act, and the Community Mental Health Act in 1963. His sisters, Eunice Kennedy Shriver and Jean Kennedy Smith, each made major contributions to the development of services for and positive attitudes toward children with disabilities through their establishment of the "Special Olympics" and "Very Special Arts" programs, respectively.

Carey told me to pay a visit to the Senate hearings and see what was going on. I did, and the hearings seemed innocuous enough to me. There were several witnesses testifying to the needs of people with disabilities, and Senator Kennedy complained about the lack of programs that provided help. At the end of the hearings, I went up to one of the staff members and introduced myself and extended friendly greetings from Carey. When I later reported to Carey, he looked at me as though I were a hopeless case and said that he had sent me over there to look things over *quietly*. Instead I had basically announced his concern and may have created slight awkwardness in his relationship with the Senator. Nothing ever came of it, as far as I know, and the hearings did not make any noticeable impact. It was not the only mistake I would make as I tried to learn the intricate and often unstated social manners of Congress and the Washington political world.

Although the elevators in the House and Senate Office Buildings were often automatic, they also had operators. Those operators, the Capital Police Force and virtually every service employee learned to recognize the faces of all 535 members of the House and Senate. When the bells rang, signaling a vote or a "Quorum Call" (a roll call to see if a legal minimum of members were on the House or Senate floors), elevators were limited to members only, and the operators recognized them on sight, asking everyone else to stand aside.

There was also the rivalry between the House of Representatives and the Senate. Clearly, most Americans were more familiar with the Senators, because they appeared more frequently on television and in the press. The two Senators from each state had a broad array of issues on which they could make their mark—anything that concerned their broad constituency. Representatives were considerably less visible. They generally served on only one or two committees and had to specialize if they hoped to make a legislative impact and gain recognition at home. When they had limited seniority, they were often assigned to the less glamorous topics, or sometimes to areas where controversies might arise.

During the Reagan Administration, for example, many members did not want to serve on the education-related committees because the President had announced his opposition to most federal aid for education and his intention to disband the Department of Education. He even wanted to repeal both The Education of All Handicapped Children Act that had passed with overwhelming, bipartisan support in 1975 and the provisions of the Rehabilitation Act of 1973 that prohibited discrimination against people with disabilities in any program receiving federal assistance. Reagan's agenda, which was bound to arouse advocates for those programs, would catch representatives in the middle between their President and their constituents in what was sure to be an emotional battle.

During the Johnson Administration, the feeling was quite the opposite; education was where the important "action" was, and representatives were eager to serve its cause whenever possible. In the process, I learned the pecking order of committees and who the more powerful members were. In the House, the Appropriations Committee was clearly the plum assignment—money talks—but I came to understand that the Ways and Means Committee was just as significant, if not more so. Because Ways and Means initiated tax bills, it was of enormous importance to the business community. Its members also had the chance to put forward legislation that would be extremely beneficial to constituents on a national level, such as Social Security and after 1965, Medicare, and so its political impact was huge.

Ways and Means had another very important political function. The Democrats, as majority members, served as "The Committee on Committees." They decided to which committees representatives would be assigned. The Speaker and Majority Leader had roles in this process where it concerned their special interests, and the Ways and Means chairman and members picked up additional influence by being able to "work with the Speaker." A few years after the ad hoc Subcommittee on the Handicapped ceased to exist, Carey was elected to Ways and Means and in his joy, explained its significance to me. When I referred to his "appointment" to the committee, he quickly corrected me. "It is an election," he said, which added additional honor as it represented the approval of his peers in Congress.

A Bigger Mistake

After the meeting at the White House indicated that H.R. 14 was not going to get Administration backing in 1966, we began to work on another piece of legislation, "The Model Secondary School for the Deaf Act," (P.L. 89-694), Once again, Patria Winalski played a key role. At the time, she was serving as Executive Secretary for the National Advisory Committee on the Deaf, a committee she helped create with

Senate counsel Jack Forsythe, and in all likelihood with the assistance of Chairman Fogarty.

The average graduates of a school for the deaf—at that time virtually the only educational opportunity available—had about a third or fourth grade reading level. (It is not much better today, due to the enormous difficulty of teaching language to a non-hearing child.) While Gallaudet University offered a liberal arts program to graduates of schools for the deaf, it had to have a special preparatory program, emphasizing language and reading. The newly created National Technical Institute for the Deaf (NTID) faced similar problems. But since it also offered diploma programs in special technical and vocational skills and Associates of Arts degrees, as well as higher level degrees, it had a range of programs with varying academic demands.

Winalski argued that creating a national model high school would fill the gap between the average achievement and college level work. She had support from several members of the National Advisory Committee, but not all. The idea was to create a residential school which would be tuition-free and open to students across the nation, and housed on the Gallaudet campus. The college's administrators supported the program, but were wary of involvement with Winalski. Her son was a student at Gallaudet, and she was a person dedicated to getting her way. (Later, the college hired her son.) She knew how to play "rough," getting her friends with power over appropriations to write certain financial requirements into bills, or conversely, leave out funds that agencies were counting on. A number of programs designed to benefit deaf children and adults, including the Advisory Committee that employed her, resulted from direct Congressional action, although the Administration had no wish for the programs in question.

The communities interested in deafness were sharply divided by educational philosophy. Most persons who were deaf, and most professionals at state schools for the deaf and at Gallaudet University, believed in using sign language and finger spelling as the primary communication tools for socialization and education. Followers of the Alexander Graham Bell Association and others, known as "Oralists," felt children who were deaf should be educated by learning to read lips (also referred to as "speech reading"). Many public and several prominent private schools followed the "oral" method. The divisions over these two approaches were deep and very emotional. Those interested in Oral Education did not welcome another federal program on the Gallaudet campus, which would employ sign language for instruction, but they were in the political minority, and so the legislation moved forward in hearings that called mostly supportive witnesses.

As I learned through tangential conversations with Carey, his enthusiasm for the Model Secondary School for the Deaf (MSSD) bill reflected not only his earlier interests in education of the deaf, (NTID and the amendment to ESEA), but also his understanding that it was necessary to give substance to his "ad hoc" subcommittee. He wanted to achieve a legislative coup that would help him keep the subcommittee going until the next Congress convened in January, 1967. He assumed that he would re-introduce H.R. 14 then with at least some backing from the Johnson Administration. I, however, had not been directly informed about these plans, other than that he hoped to keep the subcommittee alive.

I moved ahead on my own in conversations with Jack Forsythe, Charlie Lee and Roy Millenson, the top education aide to Senator Jacob Javits (Republican, NY). The Senate was still considering what it wanted to do with the 1966 amendments to ESEA. The House had completed its version. Conversations with Senate staff explored the possibility of taking several components of the Carey Bill and adding them to the Senate ESEA bill. Then, after it was passed, there would be a "conference" between the House and Senate to iron out where the bills differed. The House would have the opportunity to accept the Senate's provisions on education of the handicapped and they would become law without having to wait until the next Congress. The key provisions we discussed were the program of grants to the states, the Bureau of Education for the

Handicapped and the new Advisory Committee. The other sections of H.R. 14 could be passed later.

I was focused on getting these basic provisions into law and excited that it would provide immediate success beyond the MSSD bill. But when I told Carey what we had achieved, he was furious. While he did not say it in so many words, he clearly implied that he thought I was an ivory tower idiot. As I recall, he barked, "You have given away my bill!" Although he was right—technically it would be a Senate, not a House provision—I was dumbfounded; I thought he would be pleased to get the substance of his legislation enacted. But he insisted that he would have gotten it enacted the following year, and it would have been under his name.

I conferred with Bill Geer of CEC and told him how I had been naive and unaware of a central concept of the legislative process—the importance, politically, of being credited as the sponsor of successful legislation. Bill agreed to write to Carey, explaining that CEC recognized that the provisions in question grew out of his committee hearings and his proposed legislation, H.R. 14, and that CEC would identify the measure as "The Carey Bill" in all published references to the legislation. Further, in any ceremonies celebrating its success, Carey would be identified as the sponsor. I believe my boss was somewhat assuaged, and in fact we, and others, referred to the legislation as "The Carey Bill" in press releases and communications to the media.

The First Education of the Handicapped Act

The Senate passed the ESEA amendments and a conference with the House was scheduled. The chairmen of each committee in conjunction with the Speaker and the Senate leadership named the members of their committees who would be conferees. Generally that included the subcommittee chairmen who were most involved in the legislation and those participants who had sponsored significant portions of the legislation. Another silent selection criterion was whether the members would support the chairman in difficult decisions.

It is another example of how committee chairmen could wield significant power, amplifying their ability to assign members to favored subcommittees, schedule hearings on favored bills while leaving others untouched, and rallying members around certain legislation. Adam Powell was a very powerful chairman, exercising great authority in his committee. In addition to the majority conferees, the "ranking" minority member of the committee and the minority party leadership selected their conferees. The ranking member would, under the old seniority system, be the committee chairman if the House changed majority parties, and often cooperated on matters with the chair. Under newer systems, the leadership and the members choose a chairman rather than relying solely on seniority.

HEW's leaders were lukewarm about the disability provisions. Their main interest was on legislation that would support education for poor and minority children, and while they could not oppose aiding children with disabilities, they did not want the new programs to be significant competitors in an already scarce funding pool.

While they were tepid about disability programs, they strongly opposed the proposed Bureau of Education for the Handicapped. Having just scattered the existing programs into various larger Bureaus, they saw no reason to create a new administrative unit, especially a Bureau, whose head would report directly to the Commissioner, along with other major program Bureaus: Elementary and Secondary, Higher Education, etc.

I advocated strongly for a Bureau to Carey, against the direct arguments of HEW Secretary John Gardner and Education Commissioner Harold Howe II. I explained how destructive the recent Office of Education reorganization had been to program operations and morale, and how parents and professionals in the disability field felt let down by the current structure, in contrast to the high point in the Kennedy Administration when the Division of Handicapped Children and Youth had been formed and was well received nationally. It was at this point that the decision of the Commissioner not to appear at the hearing and the negative reaction to the testimony of Dr. Bigelow came home to roost, helping to set the stage for an action in which the Congressional majority defied the Administration of its own party.

The night before the Conference Committee, I received a call from Carey to meet him at 6 p.m. in John Fogarty's office. When I arrived, Fogarty offered me a Scotch and we sat down to talk things over. One of the "perks" of life in the House was that about 4 p.m. in the afternoon a bucket of ice would be delivered to each office. The nearby liquor store also delivered very promptly. Much business began at about 6 p.m. and continued, sometimes for many hours, with increasing conviviality, in the nearby Democratic and Republican Clubs, and in local "Hill" restaurants.

Chairman Fogarty was particularly interested in the issue of the Bureau. I assumed that the Administration had been speaking with him, asking him to influence Carey and/or Chairman Powell. I went over the issues, why we thought the Bureau was necessary and why the Administration opposed it. Carey said little, obviously having had his say earlier. Finally, Fogarty smiled and said, "You just won your battle for the handicapped, Hughie."

Carey was scheduled to speak the next evening at an event sponsored by the St. Francis de Sales School for the Deaf in his Brooklyn district. He would announce the victory there and to the New York media. He asked me to write a press release about "The Carey Bill" being agreed to in the conference and his victorious battle for a Bureau for the Handicapped. I went down to my office and prepared the release.

I had a meeting scheduled the next morning in Jack Forsythe's office with HEW's top lobbyist, Deputy Assistant Secretary for Legislation Samuel Halperin, and Deputy Education Commissioner Graham Sullivan. They were there to excise the Bureau from the bill. They offered to create a Division instead (one step down in the administrative ladder) and to include in it the research program in education for the handicapped, which they had stoutly refused until then to transfer from the Bureau of Research. I rejected all offers, although it became clear that Jack must have agreed to the division concept, (I considered it a betrayal by him and probably by Patria Winalski as well). I did not tell the HEW people or Jack about my meeting with Fogarty and Carey—I had learned some lessons by then; I just simply refused to make any changes. Later Jack told me he was astonished I didn't negotiate since it was "our" Administration and I was so new on the job. It was some years before I told him of the Fogarty meeting. (I always felt Jack was a bit jealous of Fogarty, who also had a record of doing favors for Pat.)

A Conference to Remember

Room EF-100 was in the center of the Capitol. Ritually, the Senators entered from a door on their side, and the representatives from another opposite to it. The chairman of the conference committee sat in the middle position on the long side of the table. That is a Washington tradition. When the Cabinet meets, the President sits in the middle, not at one end as is common in business and other organizational meetings. There is considerable jockeying among underlings to get near the middle next to or directly across from the "principal." In most situations, seats are assigned officially or by tradition, with the nearest to the center going to the most senior people.

I was delighted to be able to attend the conference, whose deliberations are always secret, not recorded in public minutes. After the "horse-trading" and compromises are made and all the differences agreed to, a conference report explains how each point of difference was resolved—the House conceded this, the Senate conceded that, a new provision was substituted, etc. The discussions and "horse trading" are not disclosed.

Only the senior Counsel and professional staff directly involved in the issues to be resolved were present. Eventually, "The Carey Bill" provisions came up. Carey supported the Senate provisions, explaining their origin, including the Bureau. There was some discussion from members about whether they should go into effect a year later and whether a Bureau was necessary, but it was perfunctory. When Chairman Powell said, the "House agrees," the conference moved on to other issues.

Carey left at the noon break to fly to New York, press release in hand. After lunch I decided, with considerable trepidation, to return to the conference. Since the only business in which I was directly involved had been decided in the morning, I was afraid someone would challenge my right to be there, but I decided to risk it since it was an opportunity I might not have again. (I didn't.)

I tucked myself in the row where staff sat, behind the House members, and listened as the afternoon's discussions began. Before long, one of the Democratic members surprisingly brought up the "Handicapped Provisions." He said it was his understanding that the matter of a Bureau had been put off for six months and would be considered again in the next Congress. It was clear to me that the Administration had spoken with him during the break and asked him to undo the earlier decision. Another member said, somewhat indifferently, that he thought that might be so. There was a stirring around the table as side conversations began. Across the room I could see Roy Millenson, a member of Senator Javits' staff who was a supporter of this legislation, duck out to get the Senator.

As the conversation continued and it seemed the deal for the Bureau might come apart, I had an image of Carey being mightily embarrassed in New York, so I summoned my courage and approached Chairman Powell. I was close to an interloper, but he listened willingly as I quickly told him that Carey had felt this issue was decided and was on his way to New York to announce it. Powell turned to the group and said, "This is Carey's man and he says Carey felt this was decided and is going to a speaking engagement in his district to announce it." The committee member who had suggested the reconsideration said, "That's too bad. Carey should be here. The conference isn't over."

When Roy Millenson came back in and reported, "Senator Javits thinks it was agreed to," there was little reaction around the table. Powell looked to the "clerks" who were recording the proceedings and said, "What do the minutes show?" Stewart McClure, the Senate clerk, said his minutes did not mention the specific point in question. Powell turned to Don Behrens, the House clerk, and said, "What do you have?" Behrens replied, "My notes show it was agreed to." With that, Powell said, "OK, let's move on."

I sat there taking deep breaths to calm my beating heart. I kept thinking what would have happened if the conference had made the change and how it would have affected Carey. I thought about how close I had come to not returning to the room because my presence was "pushing it."

When there was a break, I went over to Don Behrens and said, "Boy, am I glad your notes showed that was agreed to!" He looked at me calmly and said, "What notes—that's what you wanted wasn't it?" I looked at him, astonished, and laughingly said, "Is that how you make laws around here?" He replied, "That was a lot better than many other times."

The provisions on education of the handicapped became a new section of the Elementary and Secondary Education Act, Title VI. For the next several years the act was referred to in the special education community as "Title VI" and its grant provisions were known in the States as "Title VI funds." There was a phrase in the act that said the "short title" of the legislation was the "Education of the Handicapped Act," but that title did not come into common usage. Neither was it called "The Carey Act," although Bill Geer followed through on his promise and CEC publications referred to "The Carey Bill" while the Congress was acting on the provisions. Later, when President Johnson signed it into law, Carey was prominently pictured behind the President with other House and Senate education leaders and I had the privilege of shaking the President's hand and receiving one of the pens he used during the signing.

The photo session with the President and Mrs. Johnson was an event in itself. It took place in of one of the ceremonial rooms on the first floor of the White House. On the wooden floor was a white strip of tape, between the President and the First Lady. As I entered the room, a Marine guard asked for my name, and told me to stand on the white tape and shake hands. As I followed the directions, I looked straight at the President, who had turned his head slightly to his left toward the camera. Two days later I received the photograph in the mail, showing a smiling President and a good portrait of my right ear and profile. An experienced politician knew to turn his head away from the President to have his face fully shown, but I, as a neophyte, didn't have the "ill manners" not to look the President of the United States in the eye when shaking his hand.

Front row, from left: Harold Howe II, Commissioner of Education;
Rep. Hugh L. Carey, sponsor of the first "Education of the Handicapped Act;"
Rep. William Ayers, Ranking Minority Member of the Education and Labor Committee; Vice President Hubert H. Humphrey;
Rep. Harley Staggers, Chairman Interstate and Foreign Commerce Committee.
Back Row, from left: unidentified, unidentified,
John Gardner, Secretary of Health, Education and Welfare;
Rep. Carleton Sickles, Member, Ad-hoc Subcommittee on Handicapped.

Meeting President Johnson after the first
"Education for the Handicapped Act" bill signing

CHAPTER 3

The Model Secondary School for the Deaf Act

The Model Secondary School for the Deaf (MSSD) Act was small potatoes compared with a new federal law which promised to provide funds to every state for "initiating, expanding and improving" educational programming for children with disabilities. But it had political significance well beyond its educational import, and it led to my being present at one of the most momentous political events of that era.

Congressman Carey wanted to have his subcommittee complete legislation and see it into law. "The Carey Bill" did not really count as a subcommittee accomplishment, so he turned his focus to MSSD instead. As the hearings progressed, it became apparent from testimony of specialists that it was unlikely that students of high school age would come from many distant states to attend the school in Washington. It was still feasible, however, to have a regional program which would attract students from the nearby states, if the educational curriculum was exceptional and would improve prospects for success in higher education. Most of the testimony supported the concept as worth a try.

Eloise Thornberry of Austin, Texas was a member of the National Advisory Committee on the Deaf. She was married to Homer Thornberry, who was the Congressman from the Austin area and therefore was, as President Johnson frequently said, "My Congressman." Mrs. Thornberry was well known in the White House, and Carey asked her if she would put in a good word for the MSSD bill with key aides to the President. If the

White House approved, the Bureau of the Budget would not oppose the legislation, which would use federal funds to build and operate the school, and the chances for passing the bill in Congress would be much better.

Mrs. Thornberry, as a member of the advisory committee, was interested in helping with programs serving the deaf and followed up on Carey's request at the White House. It was not until the national conference on education of the deaf, held at the Broadmoor Hotel in Colorado Springs, another project for which Pat Winalski, the committee's Executive Secretary, had secured special funding from the Appropriations Committee, that the reason for Mrs. Thornberry's championing the cause of the deaf became clear. When she introduced Carey as keynote speaker she said, "My interest in the deaf came about because my husband Homer is the son of deaf parents. In fact, on our honeymoon, Homer taught me the manual alphabet." As the audience roared with laughter, she looked around innocently at Carey and the others on the dais.

One final footnote about the Thornberrys is that the President nominated Homer Thornberry for the Supreme Court at the same time he nominated Associate Justice Abraham Fortas to be Chief Justice. The Fortas nomination quickly became a political football after it was revealed that Fortas had received a speaking fee from a foundation established by a businessman whose dealings were being questioned by the Securities and Exchange Commission. Fortas was also accused of having continued to give the President advice while he was a sitting Supreme Court Justice. It was toward the end of Johnson's presidency and the wrangling finally prevented Fortas from being confirmed by the Senate as Chief Justice, and so Homer Thornberry, then a judge on the U.S. Court of Appeals, whose appointment was not considered controversial, watched helplessly as his once-in-a-lifetime opportunity to sit on the High Court passed by. (As an indication of how times have changed, it is interesting to recall the events of 2004 when Justice Scalia went hunting with Vice President Cheney. At the time, a case was scheduled to be heard by the Court, which involved Cheney's refusal to share the names of the businessmen who met with his task force on energy policy. Scalia rebuffed all calls to recuse himself when the case reached the Court.)

In his informative book, "Counsel to the President," Clark Clifford, one of Washington's "Wise Men," who served under Presidents Truman and Johnson and advised other Presidents, reports that he suggested to President Johnson that Fortas' nomination might be saved if Thornberry were replaced with a nominee more favorable to the Republicans. Clifford felt that both Fortas and Thornberry were seen as Johnson "cronies." Johnson did not withdraw Thornberry's nomination. Clifford did not speculate on why the President did not follow his recommendation. In my mind, it might have been loyalty, tenacity or fatigue in the milieu of Vietnam.

***

As the 89th Congress drew to a close in 1966, the MSSD bill was approved at the subcommittee level. The next step was to have it scheduled for consideration by the full Committee on Education and Labor. If approved there, the bill would then move to the Rules Committee, which set the guidelines for the amount and kind of debate and amendments that would be allowed on the "Floor" of the House before the final vote.. As timing was critical, we had established with the Senate Labor and Welfare Committee, through Jack Forsythe, that the Senate would pass Carey's House Bill without change, thereby eliminating the need for a conference committee.

Changing "The Rules" on Adam Clayton Powell

The man who chaired the Education and Labor Committee had been a controversial figure throughout his Congressional career. Adam Clayton Powell was the Minister of the Abyssinian Baptist Church in Harlem when elected to the House of Representatives, but he had a reputation for "high living." He was often seen in the company of pretty women and known for taking frequent trips to Bimini in the Bahamas.

There were charges brewing that he "padded" his office and committee payrolls by employing friends and had misused Congressional funds. Many, including his supporters, believed that these charges were generated in large measure by jealousy, hypocrisy and racism. While Powell may have been something of a scoundrel, it was not at all clear that he acted very differently than other senior members of Congress who were not the target of charges.

In my limited contacts with him, I found Powell to be highly intelligent, sophisticated and obviously attractive to women. As chairman of the Education and Labor Committee, he had for years added his "Powell Amendment" to every potential education bill, disallowing federal funds to flow to segregated schools. Southerners would not agree to any bill with the Powell Amendment on it. After the Civil Rights bills passed early in the Johnson Administration, the Powell Amendment was no longer necessary. His reputation with Carey and others in the know was that he had done a masterful job in securing passage for the President's education- and job-related programs.

One night he and Powell's chief aide, Chuck Stone, invited me into his boss's office for an "after 6 p.m. Scotch," and we chatted a bit about the disability legislation I was working on. At one point the Congressman looked at me, smiled and said, "They say I'm too race-conscious, but how can they say that when I have a professor from Alabama on my staff?"

There was a movement within the committee to change the rules of operation, which would strip Chairman Powell of much of his power. The new rules would establish six subcommittees, chaired by the members with the most seniority on the committee. The chairman could not create ad hoc committees or special task forces without the approval of the entire committee, nor would he be able to appoint his candidates to chair the standing subcommittees.

By the time this transfer of power was complete, the subcommittee chairmen were more conservative on a number of issues than Powell or the Administration, and they could—and later did—join with the

Republican members for a majority on certain issues. At the same time, there was a similar movement in the House to strip Powell of his seniority, and thereby his chairmanship, and to have him expelled. The vote on ousting him from his elected office was to take place when the House reconvened in January of 1967.

Unfortunately for the MSSD bill, we needed to get committee approval at the same meeting that would challenge the chairman's powers. At Carey's direction, I circulated our bill and the accompanying "report," which I had prepared to explain its features and anticipated costs, in accordance with the committee's rules requiring a two-day period of notification prior to the meeting.

There was a quite a bit of backstage dealing going on. Meanwhile, busloads of Powell's constituents came down from Harlem and gathered in the ornate marble halls of the Rayburn Building outside of the committee room, voicing their support for the chairman and their outrage at the proposed changes.

When the committee met, besides the members, only its general counsel, Jack Reed, and I were present. Later, Charlie Radcliffe, counsel for the Republicans, was admitted as well. My only reason for being there was to bring up the MSSD bill after the "main event," if that were even possible. I sat quietly to the side and hoped I wouldn't be ejected.

Members milled around the elevated dais in the committee room, but the chairman was nowhere to be seen. Meanwhile, the sounds of raised voices, sometimes in chants, occasionally in gospel song, spilled in from the halls. The tension was palpable. After 20 minutes or so, perhaps longer, Congresswoman Edith Green (Democrat, OR), one of the subcommittee chairs—she was third ranking in seniority after Representative Carl Perkins (Democrat, KY) and Representative Frank Thompson (Democrat, NJ)—decided to take command. She stood in the chairman's place, rapped the gavel and tried to call the meeting to order. A number of members in the waiting rooms just off the main room looked in to see what was happening. Perkins, who was next in seniority after the chairman, made some quiet comment indicating his disapproval, and another member—I believe it was Thompson—said, "Who died and left you in charge?" The ranking minority member, William Ayers (Republican, OH), also indicated his displeasure and the period of restless waiting resumed.

Finally, there was a loud murmur from the halls and then applause as Powell neared the room. He entered from the side room and took his place as chairman. Immediately a cacophony of voices rang out as various members tried to be recognized so that they could put some parliamentary maneuver into motion. It was bedlam. Powell sat there, quietly lit a cigarette and slowly blew the smoke out of his aquiline nose, waiting for the hullabaloo to die down. He rapped his gavel, bringing a moment of quiet and said calmly, "If you could be ladies and gentlemen, for even a few moments, we could begin."

The debate that followed was anticlimactic. Little of substance was said, other than the introductions of motions to install new rules. A number of Republicans followed an old political adage—"Let's you and him fight"—and decided to let the Democrats quarrel among themselves rather than getting involved. Representative Sam Gibbons (Democrat, FL) from Tampa was the outspoken leader of the anti-Powell faction. The subcommittee chairs who had the most to gain from the changes voted for their interests and in a relatively short time, the new rules were adopted and the first step, a huge one, toward Adam Clayton Powell's fall from power was accomplished. (In January during the next Congressional session, the process began in which he was stripped of seniority by the House and expelled. This was followed by his reelection, but Powell did not regain his seniority and committee chairmanship, and he seldom attended the committee or House sessions before retiring).

After the dust settled, Carey attempted to bring up the MSSD bill, explaining that while it was untimely, the rapidly approaching end of the House session required committee action as soon as possible. Congressman Ayers objected, saying that proper notice was not given under the rules of the committee. Carey replied that I had circulated the bill and report more than 48 hours earlier, as required. Ayers didn't have a bone to pick with Carey—he was angry at the attack on Powell and on the traditions of seniority and chairmanship, which would have served him if Republicans became the majority—but stated that since the new rules had just been adopted, the 48 hours had to begin then. Powell adjourned the meeting.

"The Deaf Will Be Glad To Hear That"

That week during a debate on the House "Floor" on "The Poverty Bill," Carey made a comment about some people lacking compassion for the handicapped and poor. Ayers, who was on the opposing side, asked for the floor. He explained that "the gentleman from New York's" reference was brought about because a procedural rule had been followed which required his bill for a high school for the deaf be considered by the Education and Labor Committee at a later time. Ayers went on to assure Carey that he had no objection to the substance of the bill and would support it when it came up under the new rules. Carey, gratified, and never at a loss for words, replied, "The deaf will be glad to hear that."

One of my jobs was to read the remarks made on the floor concerning our legislation and correct any grammatical or factual mistakes before they were printed in the "Congressional Record." That was and continues to be standard practice. I decided the remark, while possibly offensive to some, should become part of Congressional history.

The next week the MSSD bill was approved in committee and sent to the House floor under an expedited procedure that required unanimous consent to be considered. We had concerns about certain "gadflies," who objected to virtually every bill.

One particular gadfly we worried about was Representative H.R. Gross (Republican, IA) who often blocked bills needing unanimous consent. In one memorable exchange on the floor of the House, Gross objected to the Office of Education scheduling a conference on Title III of the Elementary and Secondary Education Act in Hawaii because of the travel costs. Gross asked, "Why can't they have the conference in the United States?" Representative Patsy Mink (Democrat, HI) politely informed the "gentleman from Iowa" that Hawaii had become the 50th state some years before.

In this case, no one objected and the bill, after passage by the Senate, was sent to the president. Once again we happily visited the White House and watched as President Johnson signed the bill into law. I did not get another photograph of my ear, or of the President.

PART TWO

The Bureau of Education for the Handicapped and Federal Policy in Special Education, 1967-1975

Was the "battle" to create a Bureau for Education of the Handicapped (BEH) in the U.S. Office of Education worth it? The actions of a federal agency, even a significant one like a bureau, are generally invisible to all but a few who follow the subject area closely. That is, unless it is the Federal Bureau of Investigation with its relentless media machine glorifying its exploits, especially those of its chief at the time, J. Edgar Hoover.

During the period of 1967 to 1975, many new federal programs began to support services for children with disabilities. They were passed by Congress essentially one at a time and each group affected—parents of deaf and blind children; people concerned about education for preschool children—was very aware of the new laws. Many realized that BEH was involved in administering the programs, but few understood that the impetus for the legislation often came from the Bureau by way of the Congress.

BEH's low profile was a normal aspect of the process: Congress passes the bills and the President signs them into the laws. In an electoral, political process, they are proudly at the front and center, and they should be. It is not unusual for a Congressman back in his district to "announce" each new piece of federal funding that arrives there, whether he had anything to do with it or not. The White House makes sure that Congressional members of its party get the news of the release of funds before anyone from the opposition or the media.

BEH did, however, play a critical role in the development of public policy in the education of children with disabilities, and this section recounts some of those activities.

CHAPTER 4

From "The Hill" to "Downtown"

The Washington world most closely affecting special education changed dramatically in January of 1967 because of two remarkable events. John Fogarty, who chaired the Appropriations Subcommittee for Health, Education, Welfare and Labor was found dead in his office just as the new Congress was convening, and Adam Clayton Powell was stripped of his seniority and the political battle over his expulsion from the House of Representatives began. With the support base for the ad hoc Subcommittee on the Handicapped gone, it soon after ceased to exist. Representative Carl Perkins (Democrat, KY) became the new chairman of the Education and Labor Committee, and the standing subcommittee chairs wanted all legislative issues assigned to themselves.

There was a period of days when Carey, grieving over the loss of his close friend and mentor, tried to negotiate to save the subcommittee, but he did not succeed. Without telling me, he also spoke with Chairman Perkins about adding me to the staff of the full committee as one of the 10 professional staff members. I would play the role of the education specialist.

Each of the six subcommittee chairmen wanted a representative on the full committee staff in addition to the regular appointed staff members, so the competition was intense. I was on good terms with a number of the current committee staff and with several of Perkins' key subordinates, including Jack Reed, who was slated to become counsel for the full committee. Jack, a shrewd and affable lawyer, was very able and knowledgeable in the politics of legislation and reelection.

The Committee Staff Role

There is a difference, sometimes blurred, between the roles of "office staff" and "committee staff." The former, divided between the Capitol Hill office and the home district, focuses on the priorities of and services for constituents, including, of course, getting the representative or Senator reelected.

The committee staff has to be more separate from local politics. Its members cannot go to the district to be involved in the campaign, for example, because they are paid by the committee to do legislative work. While office staff, paid by government funds, cannot be "campaign workers" either, the line is not always clearly drawn in practice, and a certain amount of ambiguity is tolerated.

When the need for a local presence arises, as it sometimes does, the staff member in question may resign or take leave from the committee staff for the duration of the campaign. Office and committee staff members realize that without a representative in Congress, they have no job, so virtually every legislative decision is weighed in terms of political effect. One example, common in relation to education legislation, was the development of the formula for distributing education funding. Representatives from wealthier suburban areas liked formulas based on population figures and local in-kind spending. Members from rural or poorer districts wanted weighted formulas that added extra funds to compensate for their situation. Battles of this kind were part of the process for virtually every bill as it developed.

Carey obviously hoped that with me on the committee staff we could pursue our legislative agenda—a more comprehensive Carey Bill for aiding children with disabilities. I appreciated his recommending me; it was a mark of respect and loyalty. While Carey was often gruff and did not provide much positive reinforcement, his desire for my becoming a committee staff member was more than just a matter of protecting his interests. It was a way of showing that actions spoke louder than his gruff words or absence of positive feedback. While we might not have a subcommittee, he could take a leadership role if Chairman Perkins was willing to consider Carey's legislation in the full committee, and I would do the staff work necessary.

Working for Carey meant having to deal with his style. He was bright and a quick study—he retained factual information very well. He was utterly captivating over drinks in the Democratic club and always charming to my wife and others in social situations. He was also perfectly capable of leaving you standing in front of his desk for several minutes after you had been summoned while he continued to read or sign materials. He did not feel it necessary to acknowledge your presence.

His secretary in the Capitol Hill office, Mildred, was cut from his gruff cloth. She had a reputation among other Congressional staff, maintenance workers and delivery men of being a shrew. She seldom, if ever, smiled and perpetually signaled with her body language and curt remarks that she was "put upon." In fact, her job was no bed of roses. Not only was Carey unlikely to give compliments, but he was very hard to find, requiring her to spend an inordinate amount of time trying to track him down. When found, he was usually not grateful. The word was that Carey had been encouraged to hire her because of her previous employment with former Governor Lehman of New York. In any event, there was no office romance between them.

I had become frustrated with Carey's conduct just before the Model Secondary School for the Deaf bill was being considered in the committee and confronted him. I told him that I was not happy in the role of an ill-treated servant—that I was a professional—and would be happy to return to the university. He said little, offered no apology and commented that perhaps I was too sensitive: Washington was a tough place. A few weeks later he told me the "report" I had written on the MSSD bill to explain its purposes to the rest of the committee was "the best he had read." I took that to be an apology.

Given our history, Carey's efforts to secure a position for me on the full committee staff took on a great deal of additional significance.

Jack Reed called me into his office and told me I was being considered for the 10th and last spot on the committee staff as a professional education consultant. When Powell was chairman, Dr. Eunice Matthews had served in a similar function, but I had observed that her role had been mostly symbolic. My background as staff director made me somewhat more rooted in the practical activities of Congress and legislation.

Jack arranged an appointment with Chairman Perkins, essentially "a courtesy call." We chatted briefly about my background, but had no substantive discussion about any issues. Perkins did make it clear that I could expect the position would be offered, if somewhat obliquely—not an unusual occurrence in Washington.

I had given the possibility several days thought and felt inclined to take it, if offered. It would mean becoming involved in a broad range of education legislation, not just disability; and while my background in speech pathology and psychology did not make me much of an education expert, I had learned how the process of legislation worked and knew how to find experts when needed. I also had a working knowledge of the Office of Education from the time I had spent there in 1965 and had kept my contacts current during the Carey hearings. I knew the basics of how the federal administration of programs worked, and I welcomed the opportunity to continue my "post-doctoral program" in public policy, although I didn't consider it as a permanent career choice. I would need to ask the University of Alabama for a continued leave of absence, perhaps for another two years.

A funny thing happened between my meeting with Chairman Perkins and my career as "Tenth Man." When a new chairman is appointed, previous staff has no tenure and most or all have to find new jobs. That is the normal course of events on Capitol Hill. In this case, however, the staff members about to be dismissed had worked for Chairman Powell, and a number had been African Americans. The new staff would have none, and with Perkins being from Kentucky, there were mutterings about a "Southern" takeover and purge. So a decision was made to retain one Powell staff member, who took the "Tenth Man" position.

I was not really upset by this turn of events, because I knew Powell's staff and there were a lot of good people on it who deserved the chance to stay. Besides, this was a learning experience for me, not a career. I was on leave and could easily and happily return to university teaching. Unfortunately, my "replacement" turned out to be a symbolic appointment. The former administrative aide to Powell had her own power-base, but no substantive knowledge of education.

The next day or so, I received a call from Graham Sullivan, Deputy Commissioner of Education. Although he and I had fought over the creation of BEH, he and I had a cordial, if limited, relationship. Sullivan, an affable Californian was an experienced mover behind the scenes, working well with the Commissioner, the charismatic Harold "Doc" Howe II, who was a member of the "Eastern Establishment." (Howe went to the Ford Foundation when he left the government.) Sullivan told me that they were staffing the new BEH, and that "Doc" Howe had asked James J. Gallagher from the University of Illinois to become the Associate Commissioner and Bureau Director. He set up an appointment for me to meet with Howe to explore my becoming the Deputy Associate Commissioner, the number-two man in the BEH. In "Hill-speak," any job in the Executive Branch meant going "Downtown."

During the meeting, I felt that Howe was somewhat guarded. I think my relationship with Congress made him uncomfortable, and he was almost certainly being urged to hire me by both the House and Senate Education Committees. Another factor may have been that we had not known each other in "establishment" education circles—no surprise, there: I did not belong to the establishment. As it turned out, we developed a polite, respectful relationship. I suspect this was in large measure because his priorities revolved around Title I of the Elementary and Secondary Act and its mission to provide "compensatory education" to poor and minority children, while I was fiercely advocating for more funding for children with disabilities, many of whom belonged to the same category.

Howe was not the only education policy maker who considered the programs for children with disabilities as worthwhile, but less significant than the programs he favored. Over the following years they were seen by a number of people as competing with one another. As the Vietnam War escalated, social programs were fighting for a shrinking share of the "butter" part of the "guns and butter" funding.

James J. Gallagher

I knew "Jim" Gallagher only by reputation. He was the number-two man to Sam Kirk at the Institute for Research in Exceptional Children at the University of Illinois, where they had co-authored the best-selling basic text for beginning students of special education. Gallagher was an extraordinary educator whose competencies and interests spread across the entire range of academic proficiency, from children with mental retardation to children who were gifted and talented. His writings ranged across this spectrum and he was respected for his overall vision of special education. Later, after he left the Office of Education he became the director of the Frank Porter Graham Child Development Center at the University of North Carolina. His leadership in the movement to start infant and early childhood programs for children with disabilities had a major impact in North Carolina and across the nation.

Jim Gallagher and I hit it off from the start and we sketched out a working relationship even before he came "on board" in July. (Maritime government-speak for beginning work had made its way even into the "domestic" agencies.) As his deputy, I would handle the Congressional relations, help build new programs and greater funding, and supervise a number of administrative details. He would focus on agency mission and building a relationship with the education "field." He also turned out to be an effective, hands-on administrator who carefully oversaw the Bureau's grant programs. As a team, we worked together on quality control.

I started work at the Bureau in February as a temporary "expert" in the disability research program, where there was a vacancy. I could not be acting director until my appointment as Deputy Associate Commissioner wound its way through the civil service vetting process and the FBI found me no more than acceptably subversive. My appointment was based on training and experience, not politics, something that stood me in good stead in the years to come. As a result, I was not vulnerable to many political pressures or even changes in the politics of new Administrations. With a Ph.D. in a relevant field, administrative as well as teaching credentials at a university, and experience as director of a House subcommittee, I had no trouble meeting the civil service requirements for an executive position in the education area. I was eventually appointed to what was called a "supergrade" position, GS 16. Gallagher, as associate Commissioner, became a GS 18.

I helped out in the Division of Research, assisting one of its branch chiefs, Max Mueller, by reading proposals and preparing them for "field review" by experts outside of government. At the same time, I began to play a role in informally reviewing programs and problems with the staff, planning for the future, and keeping a liaison with Congress. Until Gallagher arrived, the official "acting director" was William Rioux, an education administrator who was not a special educator and had been "detailed" to BEH. Rioux filled the role professionally, doing what was necessary in an orderly and prompt fashion, and with the recognition that his role was temporary. I can recall no major difficulties that arose during the transition.

CHAPTER 5

The Significance of the Bureau of Education for the Handicapped (BEH)

My four-month stint in the Office of Education (OE) in 1965 and the continuing conversations I had with the people who manned the federal programs prior to the establishment of BEH—most of whom were experienced special educators who had worked in university or state and local programs—convinced me that special education would continue to get "lost in the shuffle" without a strong and visible organization. That was the reason why I had advocated so persistently for a bureau during the Carey Committee days, rather than accept the Administration's offer of a division, which would have less clout.

That view found favor in Congress, reflecting the experiences members of various committees had with government programs. While administrators preferred fewer organizational units and structures where newly emerging areas could be "controlled," legislators knew that if they wanted to give a program special priority—whether it was research on cancer or a particular military project within the Department of Defense—it would be more likely to succeed if they also created a separate organization to administer it.

When smaller programs and emerging priorities are assigned to larger agencies, in order to grow they often have to compete, with limited success, for resources, and they don't come into their own until they become independent. The structure of the National Institutes of Health (NIH) demonstrates that pattern as separate institutes have been established for such special interests as cancer research, neurological diseases, mental health and others. Each was initially part of a more generalized parent agency and tended to "get lost in the shuffle." That became especially important when money came into play. As a bureau, we could present programs for special education at high-level meetings of the Office of Education and the Department of Health Education and Welfare, where agency goals and priorities were determined and the budget deliberations took place. Further, the decisions on grant programs were approved at the bureau level and reflected the professional judgments of special education professionals rather than being filtered through a system dominated by other interests. When Gallagher or I attended such meetings, we presented a full rationale for why our programs needed funding. They were not just an add-on to the main agenda of a bureau like Elementary and Secondary Education. To put this in perspective, if you, as a Bureau Chief, have a $2 billion program of compensatory education, and also a $15 million program of special education grants, and only a limited amount of time and a limited number of budget victories to count on, what project might you pass over quickly, if you mentioned it at all?

Regional Conferences

Jim Gallagher wanted the special education field to be involved, from the start, with the new Bureau. One strategy for achieving that was to hold a series of conferences around the nation where local people involved in disability education could meet the leaders of BEH and discuss ideas and priorities. One indication of how seriously Gallagher took these meetings was that he brought all of the top leadership with him. We used to joke in self-deprecating fashion that if the plane crashed, no one would notice we were gone. On one trip, we had to abort a landing in Denver and as the plane shuddered, straining to gain altitude and avoid the nearby Rockies, the joke did not seem so funny.

The general response to the conferences was positive, and people from higher education, state education agencies and local schools attended and told us that they appreciated being involved with the Bureau. On our part, these conferences provided feedback for our ideas and fledgling projects. We were already at work developing several modest legislative programs that would have to find their way up the ladder of Executive Branch approval before even being considered by Congress. They included a new authority to fund Regional Resource Centers (RRC) to develop expertise in differential diagnosis of educational disabilities and explore effective teaching methods. They would not try to serve thousands of children, but instead, serve as a model for other such centers at state or county levels. We also proposed an Information and Recruitment program (I&R), which would encourage the recruitment of new teachers and provide guidance to parents on where they might find appropriate programs for their children. Another program we proposed would expand the already existing Captioned Films for the Deaf project to serve a broader population of children with other disabilities.

All three of these programs had been part of the Carey Bill but had not had the opportunity to be enacted. When we explained what we wanted to achieve with them at the regional meetings, we received many useful comments and suggestions. It helped us draft the legislation in final form and built a base of support for the legislation when it was eventually considered by Congress.

Key Staff

When it came to selecting the leaders for BEH, Gallagher called on colleagues in the field of special education from outside and within the government. They all had stellar credentials. As head of the program for grants to colleges, universities and state education agencies to support teacher scholarships, he chose Leonard Lucito, who had a doctorate in the education of special ed. teachers. Before joining the Bureau, he chaired the program at the University of South Florida.

James Moss was already heading the research and demonstration program, which had been transferred out and then was brought back into BEH from the Bureau of Research in OE. He had earned a Ph.D. at George Peabody College and done research under Lloyd Dunn, one of the most respected leaders in the special education field. John Gough, who had a background in education for the deaf, was the longtime leader of the Captioned Films for the Deaf Branch, another existing part of OE that came over to us. Frank Withrow, who became the director of the Division of Educational Services, also came from the field of hearing impairment, having earned a doctorate at Washington University and having gained practical experience at St. Louis' Central Institute for the Deaf. His new responsibilities included managing the new grants to states program under Title VI—The Education of the Handicapped Act—and overseeing the Captioned Films Branch.

Gallagher also named Michael Marge as Planning Officer, Lee Ross as Public Information Officer and Burt Weiner as the administrative or "Executive Officer." Marge, a Ph.D. in speech pathology, had had professional responsibilities in the pre-bureau days, heading the grant program for training speech pathologists and audiologists. Ross and Weiner had had careers in other OE agencies and joined BEH as non-specialists in special education.

The division directors and most of the specialists in the Bureau had similar credentials. They had earned doctorates and had spent time acquiring relevant field experience in higher education or local or state education programs. As a result, BEH was not "a bureaucracy" in the classical sense of general administrators with little background in the government programs they were managing. In fact, in my experience throughout my professional career, I never worked with a group that toiled harder, were more dedicated to helping children with disabilities, and brought about more significant advances for the field.

Program Planning and Budgeting

Besides giving priority to establishing linkages with experts in the field, Gallagher also wanted to emphasize planning in the process of directing future federal efforts. This approach fit well into the overall philosophy of HEW, where the top planners had come from the Defense Department headed by Robert McNamara. As the former CEO of Ford Motor Company, he had introduced a system there called "Program Planning and Budgeting," and his "disciples" had brought it to HEW.

Under this system we laid out a series of broad goals and specific objectives and developed strategies for achieving them. The strategies had projected costs associated with them. If we presented a set of goals and objectives, through the planning process we could then request the financial support required, if the plan was accepted by the OE and HEW leadership and ultimately the President's Bureau of the Budget (BOB, later called the Office of Management and Budget, or OMB). At each step in this process, our plan and budget competed for resources with the myriad other education and health initiatives, and ultimately the programs of the entire government. If successful, our program became part of the President's budget and was presented to Congress, where it would begin another round in the process of persuasion. Gallagher took this rational process very seriously and we worked hard to develop coherent plans for expanding federal programs of assistance to children with disabilities.

Early Childhood Education

If there was a highlight of Gallagher's two years as director of BEH, I think it was the development of the specifications for what became "The Handicapped Children's Early Education Assistance Act of 1968." We proposed this bill during our second legislative cycle, following our initial success in establishing the new authorities for Information and Recruitment, Regional Resource Centers and Captioned Films in 1967.

In the planning process, we began by gathering ingredients of good early childhood programs from staff experienced in that arena. We determined that our federal role would not be to start a broad, national service program like Headstart, but rather to create models or demonstration projects that would show early childhood education programs having a beneficial effect for children with various kinds of disabilities. With these programs established in local communities, we expected them to gather parent support, which would lead to their being replicated with state or local funds.

Those of us interested in speech and hearing disorders and deafness were already familiar with the effectiveness of such programs, although they were not widely available in the public schools. For the most part, only private agencies serving children with disabilities offered any programs. In some areas of the country, there was considerable resistance to early childhood programs. Some school officials, for example, deemed programs for children with mental retardation inappropriate. The reasoning, as explained to me by one local administrator, went something like this, "These eight-year-old children are functioning as four year olds, so what sense does it make to start with them at four?" As the question suggests, we would need to do a lot of educating to sell early childhood programs to some school officials. Gallagher settled on a program of three-year grants, which would include evaluation and dissemination phases as well as service applications. Preliminary budgets called for about $100,000 a year for an individual program that had these components. A smaller amount would be authorized for the first year, a good part of which might be used by the grant recipients on planning and implementation.

In addition to participating in the internal BEH development process, I began talking with some of my friends on "the Hill" about the proposed legislation. I was looking for sponsors who would have the "clout" to secure passage. Theoretically, if our proposal made its way through OE, HEW, and BOB and past the policy people at the White House, it would likely receive favorable treatment in Congress, since the Democrats who had control of the House and Senate and the President were members of the same party. However, in the words of the old proverb, "there's many a slip between the cup and the lip," and we might lose out in the budget battles within the Administration. Even if successful there, it could falter in Congressional committees and take as much as an extra year to finally receive approval. But if powerful members of Congress adopted the legislation as their own, the probability for success was great, and might happen more rapidly, which was my goal.

The Iron Triangle

Officially, I was not permitted to contact Congress on such proposals. The legislation had not yet been approved as part of the President's Budget and Legislative Proposals; and even if it had, HEW had the responsibility for Congressional contacts through its Assistant Secretary for Legislation and the relevant staff at HEW and OE. In the real world, however, federal programs have their advocates in Congress and a great deal of legislation is developed by what is known as the "iron triangle," which consists of Congressional staff, officials from the Executive Branch whom they trust, and lobbyists from the field.

When this process leads to favored treatment for big business, I have the same reservations President Eisenhower had about the military-industrial complex. Lobbyists from the chemical industry, for example, working with Congressional staff and friends in the Environmental Protection Agency to write legislation permissive toward their pollution rub me the wrong way, but when it concerns new programming for children with disabilities, my value system becomes more flexible. From 1967 to 1981 under both Democratic and Republican Presidents I worked my part of the iron triangle as a program official from the Executive Branch, and during those years every piece of legislation passed by Congress in the special education area evolved this way. In some instances, for example with PL 94-142, "The Education of All Handicapped Children Act," I worked for the legislation behind the scenes while the Nixon and Ford Administrations opposed it.

Using the "Bully Pulpit"

Before we get to the ins and outs of the proposals in question, permit me to provide a little more context for the way things get done in Washington. In 2005 I was listening to the then Surgeon General, Vice Admiral Richard Carmona, being interviewed on National Public Radio. I was astonished to hear that he seemed to be saying that he had no real power to make things happen. His approach was in vivid contrast to that of former Surgeon General Everett Koop, who became well known as a fighter against tobacco use. I felt that he should not hold that position, or perhaps that he had been appointed by the Administration with the proviso he was to suggest nothing that would cost money. His situation is instructive for one wanting to think about the possibilities for leadership in a federal role, such as his, or as a Bureau director, Assistant Secretary, etc. My own instincts and experiences ran directly counter to his statements, and I believe my approach was similar to that used by "successful" government officials.

In 1966 when I was working for Carey, one night he told me to meet him in the office of John Fogarty (Democrat, RI), then chairman of the Appropriations Subcommittee for Health, Education, Welfare and Labor. Fogarty introduced me to Dr. Stanley Yolles, who was then director of the National Institute for Mental Health (NIMH), and asked him to tell me what he had prepared for his testimony before the appropriations subcommittee the next day. The unspoken message to me was essentially: This is a model for you. Yolles asked me if I knew what the leading causes of death were for teen-aged youth and went on to mention suicide as one of them. I believe it was second after automobile accidents, but the point was that he was going to tell the Fogarty subcommittee that it was an issue which deserved their attention and that NIMH wanted to develop a prevention and treatment program.

I understood that such a proposal would make for an interesting hearing and that it would provide the committee members with an opportunity to address a problem that most people did not know existed, but that they would quickly see as worthy of federal support. In other words, it was a good idea and it would sell in Peoria.

As Surgeon General, Vice Admiral Carmona either did not understand the levers of power, or did not want to use them. With his resources in the medical community, colleagues, friends, or with help from the NIH, he could have easily identified priority issues—for example the potential threat from a flu pandemic. (When that issue later became significant and warranted action, I do not recall the Surgeon General being recognized as the leading advocate.)

He could have used his position and the "bully pulpit" first cultivated by President Theodore Roosevelt, to alert the public to the problem or spoken to a key Senator or Representative, and Congress would have quickly picked up the idea. There would have been a hearing with him as the leading witness, the ranking health officer in the government.

If the Administration did not want to spend more money on health—Bush preferred to cut taxes and had a war to pay for—the Surgeon General could have avoided saying "extra money" or "a new program" by referring to existing efforts. He also simply could have said, "More needs to be done." Such a response would have served the public interest while putting the members of Congress leading the effort and the Surgeon General's office in a positive light.

Perhaps I was fortunate that I learned that lesson from Stan Yolles early in my government service. I certainly used it many times over 16 years to develop federal policy as a staff consultant, Bureau director and Assistant secretary.

"The Hill" Staff

The key for contacting legislators most effectively is by approaching their committee staff. When we were trying to get the BEH initiatives off the ground, in the House of Representatives, the Select Subcommittee on Education, chaired by Representative Dominick Daniels (Democrat, NJ), would consider emerging legislation. The Counsel to the subcommittee was Dan Krivit, and he and I became friends. When I spoke with him about the Early Childhood Bill, he said that "Judge Daniels," as the chairman was known by intimates because of his earlier service as a judge in New Jersey, would sponsor it.

On the Republican side, the Counsel for the Minority, Charlie Radcliffe, was a friend from my days on "the Hill." Although Radcliffe was a New Hampshire conservative, he felt helping disabled children was a legitimate federal role (he believed helping poor children was another). The subcommittee also had a junior education staff member, Marty Lavor, who quite unusually, had a background in special education.

Radcliffe and Lavor worked closely with Representative Albert Quie (Republican, MN), the senior minority member on the Education and Labor Committee. Quie, a hard-working, intelligent man, was highly respected by members of both parties for doing "his homework," and he would be a good bet to favor the idea. When the time was right, I planned to speak with the Republican staff, but I knew that because we operated in the world of politics, I had to pick the right moment—when Chairman Daniels was ready to seek bipartisan sponsorship.

In the Senate, I expected to work through Jack Forsythe, Charlie Lee and Roy Millenson on the Republican side. As I was about to contact them, I received two fortuitous phone calls in short order. One was from Art Dufresne, who worked for Senator Winston Prouty (Republican, VT). The other, a few hours later, came from Wilbur Cohen, the Undersecretary of HEW, a man I admired very much for his long and effective advocacy for Social Security and Medicare. He and the chairman of the House Ways and Means Committee, Wilbur Mills (Democrat, AK), were known as "the two Wilburs," and they were the indefatigable, and ultimately successful, architects of many improvements in Social Security and of the passage of Medicare.

The Prouty Bill

Dufresne told me about a grant request for a program serving young children with mental retardation in Brattleboro, Vermont, which had been approved by the Division of Mental Retardation in the Public Health Service. Before the program could be funded, the division was transferred to another HEW agency, the Social and Rehabilitation Service. Unfortunately for Brattleboro, the money for the division stayed in the public health service, so the grant could not be made. Dufresne wondered whether we might have a program to fund the proposal. I told him we would review it under our research and demonstration authority and see if it might qualify.

While we were in the process of locating the Brattleboro proposal, Wilbur Cohen called. He also told me the same story and asked if there were some way we could help. I did not find it necessary to tell him about Dufresne's earlier call, just assured him we would look into it.

Max Mueller, the number two man in the Research Division of BEH, found the Brattleboro proposal and after examining it said it was for more of a service program than a pure demonstration project. It had, however, been approved by field reviewers in the Boston region of HEW. Mueller thought it was possible to fund it on its merits given its previous outside review.

Senator Winston L. Prouty was a key member of the Education Committee because he was a moderate Republican and well respected. His views on education and health legislation became very important because if he supported it, other Republicans would be more likely to do the same. The other leading minority Senator on the committee was Jacob Javits. While widely admired for his intelligence, he was seen by many Republicans as "too liberal," and so his support, while important, did not carry as much weight as Prouty's.

For our evolving Early Childhood Bill, this development was very good news. We could respond favorably to our Undersecretary's interest and also appeal to the most critical Republican in the Senate. In so doing, we would follow the ground rule I adhered to throughout my entire government service: Never fund anything without merit for political reasons. There were times when avoiding political decisions was difficult, but because I did it, I believe I won the respect of members in both parties and also, as it turned out, avoided significant trouble. (More about that later.) Since I wouldn't talk about pending grants with people, I also escaped being cornered in hotels during professional conventions and elsewhere by people anxious to woo a bureaucrat with decision-making power.

Art Dufresne was so pleased that Senator Prouty would be able to help his constituents support the early childhood program, that when I told him about our legislative plans, he invited me to meet with the Senator and tell him about them. We had a long and detailed conversation about our hopes to establish early childhood programs across the nation and our belief that they could help children develop more fully and reduce the severity of some disabilities.

Senator Prouty became the primary Republican sponsor of what became "The Handicapped Children's Early Education Assistance Act of 1968." Later the people in Vermont named the early childhood program in Brattleboro "The Winston Prouty Center," and in Vermont circles some called the legislation the Prouty Bill, although senior Democrats, including Judge Daniels, were the prime sponsors in the Democratically controlled Congress.[5]

***

In my years in Washington I almost never had an extended visit with a Senator about special education. Because of the general effectiveness of

---

5 Note: When I shared this memory with Jim Gallagher during the writing of this book, he recalled that he had proposed the legislation through the Executive Branch process of approval and that it was moving forward, so either process might have succeeded in getting the bill to become law. Perhaps it was only a matter of timing, with the Congressional path being more expeditious.

Congressional staff members—and I spoke with them countless times—it was not necessary for their "principals" or for me as a government policy maker, to have lengthy, face-to-face conversations. The only exceptions were the prolonged discussions of programs during Congressional hearings when I appeared as a government witness before the authorizing and appropriations committees. The direct work with Congressional staff members proved to be key for the development of most of the federal programs I was involved with during the period from 1966 to 1981, and it represents an object lesson for anyone hoping to affect public policy in Washington.

Rivalries Within OE, HEW and in BOB

There was considerable rivalry between the various federal education programs, for example, elementary and secondary education, higher education and special education, because we competed for scarce resources. The struggles began in the internal OE planning and budgeting retreats, during which we sat around a big table and presented our cases before the Commissioner. He made the final decisions based not only on our arguments but the analyses of the planning and budget specialists.

Then we competed again at the HEW level where the Secretary made the decisions. In each case, staff advisors at the top level—as opposed to "line" officers like me, who were program administrators—had strong opinions of their own that reflected priorities they had or felt their superiors should have. The fact that they had "proximity" to Secretaries, Commissioners and budget specialists, a most valued Washington commodity, gave them considerable influence. After HEW proposed its budget, they would go to hearings at the Office of Management and Budget and make their case before the budget analysts there, as did the program leaders. As might be expected, these negotiations did not always breed goodwill among the opponents, which sometimes marked future dealings.

An example of how awareness of proximity affected policy discussions occurred at a top-level staff meeting in HEW when Eliot Richardson was Secretary. Richardson was an academic at the core, and he came up with an idea for an intergovernmental program that would provide training to create new leaders in education, health, public policy, etc. He wanted to tap funds from the existing programs in these areas to pay for the program.

I happened to be at the planning meeting—not a usual thing, but something that happened occasionally as the subject warranted. All of Richardson's key staff was gathered around him at the center of the table and across from him, including members from planning, budgeting, legislative, legal counsel, etc. As they all enthusiastically greeted this idea, reinforcing his interest, I decided to be a contrary voice from the outer reaches of the table. Mr. Secretary," I began, drawing immediate scowls from the insiders. "I think there may be some problems with that idea on the Hill. Each committee up there is very protective of its turf, and I don't think any of them will want to take money away from their programs." Immediately a number of voices were raised in protest, but Richardson, quieted them, thought for a bit, and said, "I think you may well be right, Ed." The program would have been a highlight at Harvard, but it did not fly and Richardson understood that and did not push it.

The political science version of evolving legislation begins with the White House and its agency appointees developing bills with Administration approval for Congress to pass. If the President and Congress leaders are of the same party, the legislation is essentially fait accompli in most cases. What is more likely is that while the top dogs are communicating, policy is being made at a more basic level—constituents, lobbyists, federal program heads and congressional staff working together. It is like an old vaudeville sketch, Jim Gallagher used to recall: On the stage is a piano player facing the audience and playing. When he stops playing the audience applauds vigorously. So he smiles and plays more. Behind him is a striptease performer taking off her garments. When he stops playing she stops stripping. And so it goes.

By the time we faced the appropriations subcommittees, we were all generally frustrated, but I found a successful strategy of testimony: involving the members in discussions, often by giving them examples of programs in their districts or states. From my own experience as a House staff member, I knew how boring formal testimony could be and tried to "liven things up" by including anecdotes and practical examples. I knew our programs well and answered all questions myself in contrast to some other program heads who called on subordinates when they needed detailed answers.

For whatever reasons, the hearings were generally convivial and took time. Happily for our side, our requests were never cut and were often increased above the President's requests. That irritated the competing program officers, who would grumble about my taking too long. Not surprisingly, their grousing did not diminish our joy one bit at having had a successful hearing. Once on the way back to the Office, Commissioner Ted Bell showed me a slip of paper the committee chairman, "Dan" Flood (Democrat, PA) had passed him on which he'd written, "This guy is good."

I admit to overdoing it at times. At one hearing, after I mentioned examples of appealing programs in the districts of a number of committee members, the chairman, Representative Flood said facetiously, "Tell me, Dr. Martin, do you have any projects in areas that are *not* represented by members of this committee?" I replied in kind, "Not yet, Mr. Chairman, but when we get more money we intend to spread out."

Through that process I came to know the House subcommittee members, particularly Chairman Flood and the ranking minority member, Robert "Bob" Michel,(Republican, IL). That made it more possible for me to speak directly to these men if the occasion presented itself and helped with appropriations. It also involved my getting to know Ralph Vinovich, Michel's administrative assistant. Later, when Michel became the Republican Minority Leader of the House, Vinovich continued to be his number one man and helped me on several occasions. On Flood's staff, Steve Elko played that role. Knowing these two key staffers meant I could get access to present ideas and budget requests. Both Flood and Michel invited me to speak in their districts, which I did, expounding about the need to guarantee education for all children with disabilities, and mentioning the Congressman's support for programs that helped them. It wasn't campaigning in a literal sense—my remarks were on professional topics—but there were usually stories and photos in local papers (the bread and butter of grass-roots politics).

Over the years, I went to districts for Representatives or states for Senators on six or eight occasions, so it wasn't an everyday occurrence. I actually spoke for more Republicans than Democrats, despite my political leanings, because they supported special education programs. Local groups, or in some instances, a national organization such as the Council for Exceptional Children, would ask me to attend a local conference, or a ceremony honoring a Congressman or Senator for his efforts on behalf of children with disabilities. Legislative politics, like life in general, is often a person-to-person matter, and I welcomed the chance to have personal contact rather than rely solely on appearances before the committees. I also carefully avoided any partisan favoritism, which worked in my favor as the years went by and Administrations and the Senate changed party control. I headed the BEH under Administrations of both parties. (The House did not become Republican until later, after I left Washington.)

Mary Switzer

Because they saw me as trustworthy—I did not play "games" with federal funds or mislead them about prospects—both Republicans and Democrats offered me support in later years when it was needed. Mary Switzer, the long-time and highly effective head of the federal government's rehabilitation programs, was known for visiting projects on site and when she liked them, often when in key congressional districts, she invited them to submit a proposal to her agency. Not surprisingly, it was usually funded.

Switzer was a visionary who worked with Dr. Howard Rusk, the physician known as the "Father of Rehabilitation Medicine," to create a significant federal program and, in many ways, the very field of Vocational Rehabilitation. The agency she headed was called the Vocational

Rehabilitation Agency (VRA) and later was named the Rehabilitation Services Agency (RSA). Still later, as the term "welfare" came into disrepute, Switzer convinced HEW to create a new program, The Social and Rehabilitation Services Administration (SRS) and fold "welfare" programs into it.

After SRS was formed in 1967, Switzer invited me to her office for a chat and suggested that I bring the BEH over to the new SRS, (Congress would have had to agree). She told me that she admired my efforts and would like to have me on her team. I declined as politely as possible, saying that I felt the future of education for children with disabilities was to move closer to "regular" education, and such a move would go in an opposite direction. It was the last time Switzer invited me over, but I went to her funeral some years later out of respect for a pioneering woman in government and an architect of vocational rehabilitation.

One poignant memory from my meeting with her was that she had wanted the title of Assistant Secretary to go with her appointment as Administrator of SRS, which was a much larger agency than most Assistant Secretaries headed. It came with a special "flag" that she would have liked for her office. "I always wanted a flag," she told me.

When I became Assistant Secretary of Education, I thought of Mary Switzer and our conversation, but I never got a flag either—I think they had stopped issuing them—and in truth, it really did not have special meaning to me, and I never asked for one.

CHAPTER 6

An Act That Changed a Profession

The Handicapped Children's Early Education Assistance Act (PL90-538) became one of the most significant examples of how a small, federal program could alter the face of American education. Passed in 1968, it started with only $1 million for 20 planning grants of $50,000 each. Over the next decade, it grew gradually to $20 million, still a pittance for a federal program, yet its national impact was momentous.

There were a number of dimensions to this success story. First, before this federal program was enacted, only a smattering of early childhood programs for children with disabilities existed, and they were primarily supported by private, non-profit groups—state legislatures did not provide funding for early childhood education. Second, there were virtually no programs at the college and university levels to train special education teachers for this age population. Third, state agencies did not generally have certification standards in place for such teachers. Fourth, the professional literature mentioning early childhood programming consisted of only a few isolated articles. Fifth, while Head Start programs were becoming more frequent, they did not have a mandate to serve children with disabilities and for the most part did not do so. Finally, there was little current research demonstrating the value of early childhood programming for children with most types of disabilities. The few existing studies, which had been done some years in the past, did report positive results, but they had never led to the adoption of such programming.

The hearings on the legislation in the House began in the Select Education Subcommittee, chaired by Representative Dominick Daniels. To make the proceedings a bit more attractive to the members, we had arranged for the actress Nanette Fabray to testify the first day. Fabray, at the time a featured performer on the very popular "Carol Burnett Show," was very committed to working with deaf people. She had become interested in the field of deafness after she experienced a fairly severe hearing loss associated with Otosclerosis—middle ear disease—in which the tiny bones in the middle ear ossify and lose their ability to vibrate freely, which is necessary for sound to be transmitted to the nervous system and brain. As a singer and dancer, she found the hearing loss to be frightening, not to mention career-threatening. Happily for her, and many other people with Otosclerosis, with surgery, all or most of the lost hearing was restored. The experience made a lasting impression, however, and Fabray became eager to help people with hearing disabilities. Her efforts had attracted the attention of Patria Winalski, then Executive Secretary of the National Advisory Committee on the Deaf, and she was recruited to that committee.

From the professional side we arranged with subcommittee counsel Dan Krivit to invite Dr. Samuel Kirk as the lead witness. Kirk, a significant contributor to the early childhood education field, had published research years earlier suggesting that children with mental retardation could benefit from early intervention and was one of the few persistent advocates for programming that would put his findings into practice. Kirk's testimony was well received, but the subcommittee was already disposed toward the legislation, having Chairman Daniels and most members as its sponsors. The committee was most interested in meeting Nanette Fabray, and I watched as the members delighted in the opportunities to have pictures taken with her after the hearings. As the Early Childhood Act became a success, Dr. Kirk proudly mentioned to me more than once his belief that his testimony had played a critical part in making the act possible. There was no reason for me to say otherwise.

I have one lasting memory of that hearing outside the "Halls of Congress." My wife Peggy and I went out to dinner one night with Nanette Fabray (we became friends and enjoyed seeing each other over the years). As we were standing on a dark street corner trying to attract a cab, and I was waving futilely, Peggy let out an ear-shattering whistle. Nanette said, "Hey, I can do that!" and followed with a shrill blast of her own. As they continued whistling, a cab soon pulled up and I slunk out of the shadows to hold the door for the two taxi-hailing champions.

The model programs funded by the Early Childhood Act had an immediate impact. We had chosen projects that had the possibility of replication, and efforts began to duplicate successful programs by some school districts and states, and by non-profit agencies such as the United Cerebral Palsy Association, an original grant recipient. As the programs showed positive results, we decided to extend their lives beyond the original three years. (By then I was the Bureau Chief, Jim Gallagher having moved on, first to head the OE Bureau of Research and then to the University of North Carolina). A condition of the original grant was that projects were to become self-sufficient after three years, so we developed a second cycle of grants that would not support the basic service, but provided funds for continuing evaluation and replication activities, such as giving technical assistance to others, and offering training courses.

I also established priorities for funding early childhood activities under the personnel training and research programs, and any other programs that might provide additional support. Media development, regional resource centers and centers for deaf-blind children were all affected. Interestingly, not all of my colleagues appreciated the early childhood priorities. This was particularly true among some of the specialists and administrators in the personnel training program. They had become committed to a pattern of operation in which the funds were subdivided into budgets by area of disability—mental retardation, emotional disturbance, blindness, etc. The largest pot was for mental retardation training grants, and the specialists in those areas, along with the division director, Len Lucito, protected that turf ferociously. We clashed over the new priority to increase the number of people trained to work with young children and with the severely disabled on more than one occasion, and this led to my encouraging several resignations, including Lucito's.

As the years passed we saw early childhood special education emerge as a new field, based in great measure on this federal program. A professional literature developed; articles became common in the journals, and conventions included an increasing numbers of papers. The Council for Exceptional Children formed a Division on Early Childhood. Our bureau funded research projects and centers, and more data emerged. Along the way, we also discovered that we needed to strengthen the evaluation components of the projects we funded. Many had wonderful educational and clinical staff, but only a handful had members skilled in evaluation.

To meet this need we created Technical Assistance Centers. We received strong proposals for supporting such centers from the University of North Carolina, where Jim Gallagher headed the Frank Porter Graham Child Development Center, and from the University of Washington with leadership from Alice Hayden and Norris Haring. These centers employed consultants from across the nation to visit the early childhood sites and help staff develop stronger evaluation plans.

Another important result of the Handicapped Children's Early Education Assistance Act was growing communication between early childhood specialists interested in "normal" development (i.e., experts in Head Start) and the newly emerging special education professionals. This led to many joint activities, and as we tried to convince Congress to amend the Head Start Act to require that some children with disabilities be served, further collaborative projects developed.

Opening the Doors to Head Start

The involvement of children with disabilities in Head Start provides another opportunity for an insight into how Washington often works. Head Start had its own very important mandate—to help economically disadvantaged children—and it was, and continues to be, a very important and valuable service. Like other programs with not enough money to fulfill its original mandate, (e.g., Title I of the Elementary and Secondary Education Act), the administrators of the program and some of its sponsors in the Congress resisted adding a population of children with disabilities because they felt it would take resources away from their basic mission.

Hugh Carey and I had found that to be true in 1966 when we spoke with Sargent Shriver, then the director of the Office of Economic Opportunity, which included Head Start. Shriver, while sympathetic to disability education, felt the program needed to grow more before it widened its population. I believed then that it was a misunderstanding of the problem, and continue to think so today. We were not trying to add children to Head Start who were not eligible. There were many Head Start-eligible children with disabilities already. It is fair to point out, however, that serving the special needs of children with disabilities would, in some cases, be more expensive.

We pursued our programs for children with disabilities along two separate routes. In one, we suggested and Congress passed special programs like the Carey Bill and the Early Childhood Act . For the other, we convinced Congress to "earmark" larger programs such as The Vocational Education Act and Title III of the Elementary and Secondary Education Act, "Innovation and Exemplary Programs." In each case, Congress specified a portion of the funds—10% and 15%, respectively—had to be spent on programming for children with disabilities.

When we proposed following the second route with Head Start legislation, we ran into strong opposition in the House, especially from Congresswoman Patsy Mink (Democrat, HI), who was committed to the program and considered our approach an attack on its resources. Although we tried to sway her through discussions with committee staff, we did not succeed. Meanwhile, there were voluntary, cooperative efforts beginning at the local program level as early childhood specialists realized the opportunities for collaboration and assistance to additional children who needed such programs. There was no specific funding for their efforts, however.

Doris Gamser, who served as my administrative assistant, was one of my most valued friends and colleagues. She and Bob Herman, the Deputy Bureau Chief, worked with me as if we were parts of a single organism dedicated to achieving our mission come what may. We had lunch together just about every day at one of the government cafeterias and inevitably talked "business," but we didn't experience it as a burden —we felt it was a natural part of our lives. Doris, with a Master's degree in psychology, was a wonderful organizer and professional consultant on important issues. Her husband, Howard Gamser, was a likeable man and effective, too, thoroughly familiar with Congress and its ways. As former Chairman of the National Mediation Board, Howard had worked at one time for the Education and Labor Committee in the House, and he kindly offered his counsel at many difficult moments. When we faced a relevant problem, Doris would often say, "Let me talk with Howard about it."

As Bob Herman, Doris and I puzzled over how to bring Head Start into the fold, Howard and Doris suggested getting together with their friend, Ken Young, then the head lobbyist for the AFL-CIO, who was concerned with education and related human service issues. Young was a key member of the Coalition on Civil Rights, and widely respected. A lunch meeting was arranged and Doris and I met with him.

We explained our wish to see Head Start-eligible children with disabilities enjoy the benefits of that program. I told him our experience was that many such children were "Head Start rejects," as the programs felt their needs were outside of the Head Start mandate, and that we had no desire for non-poor children to dilute the Head Start funds. Soon after, we heard that Mrs. Mink dropped her opposition to our proposal and the Head Start legislation was changed accordingly. It was not earmarked for a proportion of the funding, but for a percentage of children, 10%, who qualified as children with disabilities. I considered that "victory" as a significant event, not just because of the expanded opportunity for us, but because it could unite our constituencies in support of each program.

I learned by experience and from talking with people who had helped get important programs through Congress, like Wilbur Cohen (Medicare), that Rome wasn't built in a day; and so we took smaller steps, happily, and kept coming back time and again. The strategy of earmarking existing programs was a good alternative when passing a new program of hundreds of millions of dollars for children with disabilities was not possible. Similarly, asking for help from people outside special education who knew how Washington worked, such as Howard Gamser and Ken Young, provided powerful assistance. That is what wealthy individuals and corporations now do routinely with corporate lobbyists. We had to find people with good values who were willing to help a good cause for no money. As these programs grew and became established it made the later passage of the Education for All Handicapped Children Act (PL 94-142) seem less dramatic in scope.

The Portage Project

Many of the early childhood programs became "prototypes" for others. One particularly popular model was based in the rural area of Portage, Wisconsin. It trained people who ordinarily might be deemed non-specialists—nurses, education aides and others—to work with children with disabilities as they visited their homes. In that way, parents could also receive training and carry on daily activities with the children. Because it could operate in locales where trained specialists were unavailable, the Portage project became widely replicated.

Evaluation data from Portage and similar projects, and visits from our technical assistance staff, gave us a reasonable level of confidence in the success of these programs. I phrase it that way not because we had any reason to doubt the projects, but because evaluations of such projects are not like "hard" research findings, which involve carefully controlled populations and procedures, and comparison groups. It is very difficult and expensive to conduct such research in practical field settings, but it is being done to an increasing degree with excellent results.

It turned out that the Portage project was replicated in many other countries besides the United States. Shortly before the end of the "Iron Curtain" era, an early childhood specialist I visited in Poland told me that he had begun several programs there, including a Portage project. He described a program for teaching children using non-professionals trained by the project. Even in that era of tightly controlled information, when professionals were "starved" for Western information, that message had gotten through. When I asked him if he knew what the term "Portage" referred to, he had no idea, but was greatly amused to hear that Portage was a rural community in Wisconsin. He assumed it was a technical term, not the name of a small town.

CHAPTER 7

Targeting Special Needs

The growth of public policy in special education from the passage of the Carey Bill, or more correctly, Title VI of the Elementary and Secondary Education Act—also known in shortened form as "The Education of Handicapped Children Act"—was a gradual process. Essentially we identified, in concert with people working in the field, needs of children with disabilities and suggested programs that would meet them. Examples included the early childhood programs reported on in the last chapter, as well as other specific projects discussed here.

Children Who Were Deaf and Blind

In 1968, I learned from the Centers for Disease Control (CDC), which is part of the Public Health Service, that a 1964-65 epidemic of rubella, also known as German measles, had infected many women in the first three months of pregnancy.[6]

As a result of the rubella epidemic, perhaps 20,000 babies had been born with disabilities, many of them with multiple impairments. It was estimated that as many as 5,000 children would have vision and hearing deficits severe enough to be considered "deaf-blind." They were already three to four years old and rapidly approaching the age when they would

---

6 Bob Dantona, a program specialist in the Bureau with expertise in visual handicaps, raised the possibility of a program for deaf-blind children with me, which led to my contacting CDC.

need the educational system for help. Yet, at the time, there were no more than 100 or so educational placement opportunities for children with such disabilities in the United States, most of them at the Perkins School for the Blind in Watertown, Massachusetts, and at the Alabama Institute for the Deaf and Blind in Talladega.

Working with Jim Gallagher, who was the BEH director at the time, we proposed legislation through the Administration to establish regional deaf-blind centers. They would provide some diagnosis and education and work closely with state schools and agencies to start up more localized programs. While we were certain the Johnson Administration would approve such a program, it would take considerable time, perhaps a year, to shepherd the proposal up the chain of command through the Office of Education, HEW and Bureau of Budget before White House approval.

I went to visit my former boss, Representative Carey. I felt I could count on him to introduce the needed legislation in the House. Carey, who had been having conversations with Mary Switzer, then Commissioner of Rehabilitation, was, in fact, interested in establishing a Center for Deafness and Blindness for the rehabilitation of adults. When he spoke with her about our idea, she suggested that the center, under her authority, serve both children and adults. We persuaded Carey that a single center might be feasible for the small number of adults with such disabilities—it would be more than 10 years before the "rubella" children became eligible, at 16, for vocational rehabilitation services—but that young children would be better served closer to home by our regional centers and their satellites.

Carey agreed to introduce the legislation immediately in the House and move it on a fast track. Through Jack Forsythe we arranged for Senator Lister Hill to introduce the bill in the Senate. As anticipated, the Administration agreed to support the Congressional bills, and we eliminated one year of bureaucratic wrangling.

Once the act for deaf-blind centers was passed, the next challenge was to secure funding. Again, the process of going through the Administration would be cumbersome because it had to coincide with the annual budget process. (Actually there are times when the Administration sends up "Emergency Supplemental Requests" for special consideration by Congress, but they are exceedingly rare.) Carey recommended that I should speak with Chairman Daniel Flood of the HEW-Labor Appropriations subcommittee in the House, to see if I could get the $1 million start- up funds in the current year, rather than having to wait for the next budget cycle. (Flood had replaced the late John Fogarty as chairman.) To set the wheels in motion, Carey suggested I join him and Flood for a drink at the National Democratic Club and he would make the introductions.

Soon after, Jim Moss, the director of our research division, accompanied me to the Democratic Club, where we got together with Carey, had a drink and then met Flood. We made polite conversation, waiting for the opportunity to bring up our hopes for appropriations for children with deafness and blindness, but people kept walking in, and one drink led to another as Flood, a gregarious man, visited with friends. Several hours passed and Flood suggested we repair to the Rotunda restaurant and have something to eat. That seemed like a very good idea but as soon as we got there, we were ordering not food, but another round of drinks. Flood visited with some other Congressional friends and I waited at the table.

By then my mental alertness was considerably diminished, although Flood seemed unaffected. He never came back to order dinner, and I decided I needed some fresh air—badly. I wandered outside, ambled about a bit, and resolved to go home. I am not proud of the fact that I had too much to drink, and even less proud that I drove home in my inebriated condition, albeit at about 15 miles per hour and with occasional, necessary stops. I can only add in my defense that it was the last time I ever imbibed such an amount of liquor or drove under the influence of alcohol. Then again, it was for a good cause.

I awoke the next morning with a terrible hangover. Peggy had noted my condition when I arrived home in one piece, thanking my lucky stars, and commented on my having had too much to drink. When I asked her how she knew, she said, "I think it was your crawling on the floor to the bathroom that caught my attention."

When I told her about matching drinks with Dan Flood, she asked me where Jim Moss had been. With horror, I realized that I had forgotten Jim, who was entertaining a young lady at the bar, and left him stranded 10 miles from home. Happily, as I found out later, Jim's new friend offered him shelter and so we both survived not much worse for wear. Dan Flood, to my knowledge, suffered no ill effects whatsoever.

Overcoming my acute embarrassment, I called Flood's office later that day, spoke to Steve Elko, his aide, and arranged to meet that evening. Flood and I spoke about the program at his office, and he agreed to put the $1 million in the appropriations bill. If he had noticed my disappearing act the previous night, he was gentleman enough not to mention it.

Regional Resource Centers

Jim Moss, our Director of Research, had been interested in developing a type regional resource program, (RRC), that would improve differential diagnosis and help with individualizing education. As one of our first legislative proposals, we suggested authorizing such centers, to be supported by colleges and universities, school systems or appropriate non-profit agencies.

While the Centers, we thought about ten, one in each HEW federal region, would work with actual children, they were not designed to be permanent service agencies. Instead, they would be demonstration projects, and models for the school systems, often using regional universities as sites for visiting and for instruction. The idea caught on, although a network of centers did not spread nationally. Some states combined the RRC's with Instructional Material Centers, a similar idea focused on helping teachers find appropriate materials, funding the programs through the federal funds flowing to the states under Title VI.

Information and Recruitment

Among the first programs put forward by the newly formed BEH in 1967 was one intended to provide information to parents and to recruit new teachers into the profession of special education.

The Information and Recruitment program was small. It had only a $1 million authority and no particular structure for administering the grants specified. We decided, after consulting with parents and others, to create a computerized database of programs serving children with disabilities—we were in the vanguard of making use of technology in this regard. At the time, parents were moving from community to community and state to state seeking programs for their disabled children. If a handicap was at all unique, there was little likelihood that the public schools would offer an appropriate program. Following a start-up period when the company that developed the database operated the service, a local group of parents took over and began to respond to inquiries.

To make the public aware of the existence of this computerized database, we held a competition, receiving bids from a number of public relations firms. We ended up contracting with the Robert R. Mullen Company, which, in turn, would subcontract to produce television commercials we hoped would be aired by stations as public service announcements. We called them "Closer Look" ads, and had a memorable post office box, Box 1492, Washington, DC, for inquiries. With limited resources we did little about the recruitment aspect of the program, limiting our efforts to public relations efforts.

I learned a lesson about the power of television from our attempts to publicize Closer Look. The Mullen Company arranged for me to be interviewed on the Today show, hosted at that time by Barbara Walters and Frank McGee. Walters asked me not only about Closer Look but also about funding for special education. She obviously wanted me to say that we needed more money and scolded me after we were off the air for missing an opportunity. I explained that, although it was true we needed more funds, it was not something a government official could say after the President's budget for a given year had been submitted.

The real impact of the interview was that compared to the handful of inquiries until then, we received between 20,000 and 30,000 letters in the days immediately following the show and had to "gear up" to answer all that mail.

Getting Entangled in "Watergate"

After the first year or so, the Mullen Company hired a new person to be our account executive. His name was Howard Hunt (later widely known as E. Howard Hunt). He was described to us as a former journalist for *Time* Magazine.

Our in-house manager was Harvey Liebergott, a bright, sensitive man who completed his Ph.D. in English while working for BEH. He was a humanist who, deeply concerned about our constituency, also had a realistic view of the problems faced by people with disabilities gained from teaching English at Gallaudet University, the only post-secondary liberal arts college in the world for persons who were deaf. Liebergott worked well with parents and under his leadership the program gained national impact by expanding to include giving grants to local coalitions of parents to provide assistance to similar groups in other states.

Liebergott was guarded in his appraisal of Hunt, who did not seem very imaginative in his approach to the tasks at hand, although he made it clear, inappropriately, that he was a "far right" thinker. That was no great surprise to us. We had hired the Mullen Company after they were recommended by outside "field readers" of the proposal competition, knowing that it was a firm with Republican ties and that Bob Mullen, the president and CEO, had worked in the Eisenhower Administration. It was unusual for us to have any awareness of the politics of our contractors or professional consultants, but the Mullen Company had included it in their background material, perhaps thinking that it would be a plus in the new Nixon Administration. Little did we know how close the ties to the

Administration were on the part of the new account manager with whom they saddled us.

The larger context of our activities in 1970 revolved around the newly appointed U.S. Commissioner of Education, Sidney P. Marland. Marland held a planning and budgeting retreat for the OE. During the meetings, I suggested adopting a federal "commitment" to education for every child with a disability. Marland, a former superintendent of schools in Pittsburgh, PA, had a firsthand familiarity with special education programs and was the kind of person who wanted to improve education. In my view he had a big and warm heart. He supported our plan to set a national goal of education for all children with handicaps by 1980, including our proposal for a several hundred million dollar increase in grants to the states, which were getting less than $50 million at the time.

Eventually, the Nixon Office of Management and Budget vetoed the expanded federal role, but Marland agreed that we could "call for the development of a national goal of educating all children by 1980." It just couldn't be an accepted federal goal. We made a film of the Commissioner discussing the goal and sent a copy to each of the state education Commissioners, as well as to other education policy makers, asking them to adopt this goal.

I had been asked to give a keynote speech at the annual Council for Exceptional Children convention, held that year in Miami Beach. I intended to show the Marland film, announce our "goal" and call for CEC to adopt it. In an example of man's ongoing—and all-too-often losing—struggle with technology, the projection equipment in the massive convention center showed the film but the sound was inaudible, so I jumped in and provided a kind of narration. I believe the substance came across and everyone got, as I pointed out, a sense of what films without captions were for persons who were deaf.

We felt our national goal would make a good subject for a Closer Look commercial, and Howard Hunt decided to come to Miami and set up a visit to the Mailman Center of the University of Miami. The Center was federally funded—though not by our agency—as a result of the original mental retardation legislation initiated by President Kennedy. Because it focused on mental retardation and related disabilities, we planned to take pictures with some of the children there. Later that night we were invited to a small cocktail party at the Center director's home on Key Biscayne. I was not feeling well, perhaps because of a virus or food poisoning, and I asked Howard, our designated driver, to take us back to the hotel. He proceeded to get thoroughly lost on the simple route to Miami Beach, and it took considerable time before we regained our bearings and made it to our hotel. I recovered and the ad was a success.

Some weeks later, Howard told us that he could get Julie Nixon Eisenhower to make another Closer Look commercial for us. After some deliberation about it being deemed "political," we agreed. There was something of a precedent. When Hubert Humphrey was Vice President, his wife Muriel had made a commercial for the President's Committee on Mental Retardation, also a federal agency. The ad was not seen as unduly political, although the Humphreys had a granddaughter with mental retardation, which may have reduced the political factor.

During the planning stages of the film in 1971, Robert Bennett, who was the vice president of the Mullen Company[7], called to say that Hunt was going to be working part-time in the White House. Our only concern at the time was that he would not be billed to our contract while working there, and Bennett assured us that would not happen.

The Closer Look spot was filmed without incident and Julie Nixon Eisenhower was very pleasant and cooperative. It was not released in 1971, however, and our inquiries were met with a response from Hunt that "the White House" was clearing it in a routine, if slow, fashion. Finally in the spring of 1972, Hunt said it was time to release the spot, but I said, "no." It was just months before the 1972 presidential election,

7 He soon was promoted to president of the company and later became U.S. Senator from Utah, before being defeated in 2010 at the Republican Party convention by a Tea Party-backed candidate.

and I felt the timing might cause members of Congress to think we were using "handicapped children" funds for political purposes. Hunt pursued the issue by having John Ehrlichman or an assistant call and lobby Commissioner Marland (the Commissioner left unclear who called, other than that it was in Ehrlichman's name), and I explained why I opposed the move.

I also called Bob Bennett at the PR firm, who had access to the White House Congressional liaisons through his father, then the Republican Senator from Utah. I told him I thought it was a dumb idea that was not going to help the President—who was way ahead in the polls anyway—and that it was likely to wind up in a Jack Anderson column about abuse of power. Bennett agreed and said he would speak to the White House staff. When he asked me if I wanted him to fire Hunt, I replied that I did not hire his firm to get programs for the handicapped in trouble with the White House while I was trying to get a $200 million budget increase, but that he should be able to handle Hunt without firing him.

Bennett's efforts, if there were any, did not help. In a few days Commissioner Marland had another call from the White House insisting the film be released. When I continued to refuse, he agreed that he would sign the OK and take the responsibility. As a career civil servant who did not play politics with the Republicans or Democrats, I would not put the disability programs at risk in the Congress, and as a civil servant, firing me would be a very public process. Marland had no objection to my position, but he was a presidential appointee and had to play on the team or leave.

Later that week, E. Howard Hunt was arrested in relation to the Watergate break-in, and the film was not released until after the November election. In the meantime, investigative reporters descended on me to find out why Hunt was working for us, and why there was a commercial labeled "1972 Campaign" that had been discovered in his office. Further, one of the men arrested had used the alias Edward Martinez, and that "coincidental" resemblance to my name seemed suspicious. The two most prominent investigative reporters, Jack Nelson of the *Los Angeles Times* and Eric Wentworth of the *Washington Post*, listened to my explanations and my urgings that they not write anything that would harm the programs for the handicapped. Their stories were accurate and not overly dramatic.

Hunt's involvement in the whole mess caused Boh Bennett considerable distress, especially when it was disclosed that the Robert R. Mullen Company was, in colloquial parlance, "a CIA front," which had operations in several international cities. When the company quietly closed down, Bennett went to work for Hughes Aviation, also generally regarded as a CIA partner operation. It makes clearer why the Mullen firm hired Hunt in the first place.

The final episode of this tale came when a staff member from Senator Ervin's Watergate investigation called and asked me if I was "being harassed." I replied, "Nothing out of the ordinary." I was seen as the resident Democrat (actually I was not registered by party) and had been "Acting" Deputy Commissioner for many months. In reality, I did not want to be appointed Deputy Commissioner because that would have required me to leave the civil service and take an appointment in the Nixon Administration, which I would not do. The Ervin staffer would not explain why he asked. A short time later I had a similar call from a *Washington Post* reporter. He promised he would let me know what was going on. A few days later, he came by my office and gave me a copy of a memo from presidential assistant Charles Colson to White House Counsel, James Dean. It read, "I have heard for the first time from Howard since he was arrested. He wants us to take discrete reprisals against Ed Martin and his faithful understrapper, Harvey Liebergott, who are liberal democrats of the McGovern stripe or worse." Colson added that, naturally, he had not replied to Hunt. Dean must have turned over the files to the Senate Committee.

I found out by press reports that Hunt had contacted the Cuban men who broke into the Watergate while we were all at the Miami convention.

It turned out that he had been a frequent visitor to Miami, having also been involved in the "Bay of Pigs" in some fashion or another, and had kept in touch with the Cuban-American community. It reinforced our feelings about Hunt being something of a bungler. After all, despite his familiarity with the area, he had managed to get lost between Key Biscayne and Miami Beach. It also explained why our first Closer Look television commercial, for which I had requested a Spanish language version, drew criticism from the Latino community, as it was translated in a Cuban dialect.

Closer Look was a popular program with families of children with disabilities. The commercials, developed cooperatively by Harvey Libergott and Jim Greene of the Grey North Advertising Agency in Chicago, with the assistance of skilled television directors, presented an optimistic message: "Children can be helped and should be." When parents responded, they received information and advice from other parents who manned the operation. In many cases, the pre-packaged information proved too generic, however, and those who wanted more began organizing parent support centers around the country. Martha Ziegler in Massachusetts was a leader in that effort.

The Information and Recruitment program survived Watergate and grew, helping parents across the nation. They, in turn, became active in pursuing the goal of "Education for All."

We also wanted to raise the knowledge of disability and children's needs for education and made a grant to the Children's Television Workshop program Sesame Street toward that end. Linda Bove, an actress who was deaf, began to appear on the program providing welcome first-hand experience for children with disabilities. Similarly, we also made a grant to Mister Roger's Neighborhood in support of his efforts to develop sensitivity and compassion to "differences."

This morning, as I am editing this section, the social media are filled with stories about presidential candidate Romney saying he was going to eliminate funding for PBS and "Big Bird."

Specific Learning Disabilities.

In the House, the bill received support from Dan Krivit of the Daniels subcommittee and Jack Jennings, counsel to another subcommittee of Education and Labor chaired by Chicago Representative Roman Pucinski (Democrat, IL). Daniels, Pucinski and a number of other members of the committee introduced it. The hearings in both chambers were uneventful although there was always some resistance from conservative Republicans on economic and philosophic grounds—they saw education as a state, not a federal, responsibility.

There was one memorable moment during the House floor debate, when the issue was raised about the number of school-age children with learning disabilities. We had testified that we felt it was between 1% and 3%. Pucinski, utilizing other sources, proclaimed that it was perhaps 10 or even 15%. Those figures were exactly what the opponents were worried about. As I watched from the gallery, I could see his counsel, Jack Jennings, "blanch" and move swiftly to bring Pucinski to a halt. No damage was done and the legislation passed. Soon after, for unrelated reasons, Pucinski left Congress to be elected as an alderman in Chicago, a position that carried with it a less lofty title, perhaps, but lots of patronage and local clout.

Another floor dispute involving Pucinski found him on one side of a debate over a feature of "The Poverty Bill," which was part of President Johnson's War on Poverty. The other side featured another subcommittee chairman from Education and Labor, Congressman John Dent (Democrat, PA). Their heated exchange consisted of a number of arguments, some of which were quite lengthy and convoluted. At one point, Pucinski made a telling point…which supported Dent's stance. Dent rose to the challenge and argued back, essentially bolstering Pucinski's original position. After a bit of floundering, they got back on track. Neither was known for his mastery of complicated issues.

The new Title VI section represented an important step forward for programming for children with learning disabilities. It allowed the BEH to fund a number of model projects designed to assist such children and gave national visibility to efforts to start programs at local levels. By establishing models supported by solid evaluation data, the new program also helped fight a perennial problem faced by children with learning disabilities—a tendency by some educators and policy makers to see their needs as mild and transitory. With an active federal program supporting personnel training, research and model projects, it seemed only a matter of time before children with learning disabilities would achieve full recognition under the definition of "handicapped" in the federal law.

Building a Strong Education of the Handicapped Act

Richard Smith was an attorney on the staff of the Senate Education Committee, chaired in 1970 by Senator Claiborne Pell (Democrat, RI). Pell came from a distinguished background with European antecedents and was referred to by some of the staff (not Smith) as "Wellborn Pell."

Smith had worked in the legislative office of the OE and was sympathetic and knowledgeable about federal education programs for children with handicaps. As I discussed with him one day my wish to strengthen the commitment to federal programming, he began to outline a strategy for raising the visibility of the disability programs by bringing all the separate authorities together into one large act, which would be called the "Education of the Handicapped Act." It would be on par with the "Elementary and Secondary Education Act," "The Vocational Education Act" and "The Higher Education Act." This would bring it in line with the structure of the OE, which had a separate bureau for each of these areas. The OE's resistance, starting in 1966, to having a bureau for education of the handicapped and the subsequent smaller apportioning of federal funds, had always made programs for disabled seem like, pardon the pun, "stepchildren."

While putting the various pieces of legislation into one "omnibus" bill would not dramatically increase the federal role, it would be a statement that Congress recognized that "the new kid on the block" was growing up. Public Law 91-230 brought together the original Title VI grants to the states, as well as the authorities which authorized grants for personnel training, research, early childhood model projects, learning disability model projects, service centers for children who were deaf and blind, regional resource centers, captioned films and media, and grants for public information and recruitment of personnel. Each of these programs became part of the new "Education of the Handicapped Act."

An important addition in the new act's authority was an expansion of the scope for research and demonstration to include all the various subparts, such as deaf-blind programs and early childhood programs. That way research and demonstration projects could be supported with funds from each of the several programs, increasing the available monetary resources and giving the Bureau new flexibility to create innovative projects in any area recognized as covered by the federal definition. We promptly used that authority to begin programs designed to help "severely handicapped" children and also to begin training personnel to teach them.

Many traditional special education departments had resisted the changing nature of the field, which increasingly wanted to begin programs of education for children who were severely mentally retarded, or had serious neurological/emotional disturbances such as autism. These disabilities had not traditionally been considered the responsibility of special education in the public schools, as such children were placed into state facilities or excluded from local schools. Most higher education faculties were led by people interested in higher functioning students identified as "educable mentally retarded" who were served by local schools, As a result, the faculty skills were not directly relevant to the population of the "severely handicapped."

The new legislative flexibility allowed BEH to encourage the transition from institutional care to local community programs. Later, we also gave grants to help launch an important professional organization called "The Association for the Severely Handicapped" (TASH).

We developed a strategy for trying to increase the capacity at the local level and in colleges and universities to serve these more seriously disabled children. We funded centers of excellence, called "Technical Assistance Centers," to pass along their skills and help build new training and service programs. It was similar to what we did in creating the centers for the Early Childhood program to help train evaluation skills. We called the concept "capacity building" and used it to argue for funding from the OMB. If it opposed direct funding of service programs, we would develop capacity instead.

We also hoped to develop tools for leadership and put them in place in State Educational Agencies, institutions of higher education, and other non-profit agencies. These tools included funds for hiring trained staff, special training in "best practices" developed by other professionals across the nation, development of more sophisticated evaluation skills and concepts for planning and budgeting. We felt, and the reports from the field supported the notion, that these efforts played a major role in increasing special education programming, attracting public and private funds, and spreading the impact of programs that demonstrated positive accomplishments.

A Great Party

By 1972 BEH programs were becoming more prominent and Congressional support was growing for federal special education programming. Fred Weintraub and the Council for Exceptional Children, with the help of others, I believe, decided to have a fifth anniversary of BEH celebration in one of the reception rooms of the Rayburn House Office Building.

I can never think of that building without remembering the comment of my conservative friend, Charlie Radcliffe, counsel to the Republicans on the Education and Labor Committee. As we left the building one day for lunch he said to me, "Do you see those decorations up there?" I looked up. There were several mythic figures adorning the top of the building. They appeared to be a combination of the head of horses, or horse-like creatures, blending into a cornucopia.

"That's the symbol of the Great Society," said Radcliffe, "a horn of plenty coming out of a horse's ass."

The party, however, was a great affair. Hugh Carey agreed to be master of ceremonies and a number of key Congressmen and Senators attended, saying nice things about the Bureau and about me. As we were just beginning the quest to develop what became 94-142, I was delighted with the turnout of committee members and key staff.

My wife, Peggy, stayed near the door to greet the latecomers, especially Congressmen or Senators, and bring them to the rostrum where Carey, the speakers and I sat. At some point she noticed Dan Flood, his mustache well waxed into sharp points and a black cape draped over his shoulders. She greeted him warmly and invited him in. He ignored her, standing still in the door entrance. Peggy was puzzled, but stood silently there with him.

Enjoying the BEH party with Rep. Flood, center, and Senator Harrison Williams

Carey eventually spotted him, and immediately launched into an effusive tribute of the chairman of the Appropriations subcommittee that had made these programs we celebrated possible. Then, with a flourish, he cried, "The Honorable Daniel J. Flood." As if on cue, Flood strode into the room making the grand entrance his training and inclination as an actor and leading man demanded. Peggy, an actress herself, fully understood what had transpired. Flood was not moving until he could take stage like royalty.

The parade of prominent speakers who had sponsored key legislation on our behalf continued unabated. They included Senator Harrison Williams (Democrat, NJ), the chairman of the Senate Labor and Welfare Committee, Representative John Brademas (Democrat, IN), chairman of the House subcommittee, and Representative Al Quie (Republican, MN), the ranking Republican on the House committee. Each had played a significant role in developing programs in health, education and welfare. Sadly, Williams and Flood each had troubles with the law later on, which permanently ended their productive careers.

Also at the party with Rep. Quie

John Brademas, on the other hand, was both a unique legislator in many ways and had a stellar career following his tenure in government. A Rhodes Scholar who earned a Ph.D. at Oxford, he was the first Greek-American to serve in the House, representing South Bend, Indiana for more than 20 years—no mean feat in a state generally quite conservative and Republican.

When Carey chaired the ad hoc subcommittee, Brademas had been allowed by Chairman Adam Clayton Powell to head a subcommittee-like "Task Force." Using that vehicle, Brademas championed the National Endowment for the Arts and the National Endowment for Humanities. As with the Carey subcommittee, the Task Force died when the "rules" were changed limiting Powell's power and returning all subcommittee jurisdictions to the six senior members.

Brademas' intelligence and drive led to his moving up the ladder within the leadership of the House and he became the Majority Whip, the third-ranking position in the leadership, responsible for organizing party support for legislation. After leaving Congress he became president of New York University, where he was a spectacular success, raising billions of dollars and turning that non-descript private university into a national leader in several fields, including law, business and the performing arts.

But that was all in the future. For now, the party celebrated "The Education of the Handicapped Act," pulled together by Dick Smith, and the new role of BEH as a major player on the federal education scene. We had successfully built a program, one step at a time, and the special education field and the parents of children with disabilities felt they finally had a voice in Washington.

CHAPTER 8

Captioned Television for the Deaf and Hearing Impaired

After the passage of PL 94-142, The Education for All Handicapped Children Act, in 1975, BEH had the responsibility of implementing the new law. This meant developing regulations with input from thousands of people in the field, and negotiating plans, state by state, which then had to be submitted and approved by us at the Bureau, OE, HEW and OMB. It was a massive undertaking accomplished by the hard, dedicated work of a number of people in the Bureau, who were the equivalent of offensive linemen in football—not the stars who throw or carry the ball, but the unsung heroes who put their bodies on the line to make it all possible. We will shed some light on this process in Part III. In this chapter, I want to share another specific example of the leadership that a federal agency can provide in creating an important breakthrough for a program that almost certainly would not come about in the private sector without federal support.

One morning in 1977, my telephone rang and HEW Secretary Joseph A. Califano was on the line. Actually, the Secretary himself was not "on the line," one of his assistants was, waiting for me to pick up. In Washington, as in other seats of power, business or political, there is a game played about who must pick up first on a call. When a Cabinet Secretary or the President calls, it is not really a game, and the outcome is clear from the get-go. The game is on only when people of roughly equal status clash over power.

A member of the Secretary's office staff told me one night at a party, that Califano would call out, "Get me Ed Martin." The problem was that there were two of us. The other Ed Martin was the head of the Community Health Service, while I was heading the Bureau of Education for the Handicapped. The staff wanted to avoid getting us both on the phone, one of us answering, and being greeted with something like, "Not you." They began to call me "Special Ed" and he became "Med Ed." It seemed to work, but I am not sure how.

Joe Califano—I called him "Mr. Secretary"—was a highly skilled political operator and, as the media pointed out when he left private law practice to head HEW, a very highly paid attorney. He was bright, aggressive, opinionated and determined to make a difference at the department with what he referred to as "the third largest budget in the world, after the United States and the Soviet Union."

He had been trained in government at a very high level, as an assistant in the domestic policy arena in the Johnson White House. No Administration ever had a bigger—or better—domestic policy agenda, and Califano had a reputation, like the President he had served, of wanting to get things done when he wanted to get things done. He once had me called off the 14th hole of the River Bend Golf Club in Great Falls, Virginia on Saturday because he wanted to speak with me. As I recall, a receptionist held the line while a golf cart was sent to fetch me. The Secretary wanted to "ask" me if he could move our director of public information, Lee Goodman, to his office. I, naturally, agreed and asked him when, to which he replied, "He is already here."

Later I told that story to Dick Beattie, then General Counsel, and he laughed and then told me about an experience he had. He and fellow HEW attorney, Ben Heineman Jr., (known then as the man with the best resume in Washington), were on a vacation float trip down the Snake River in Idaho. Suddenly their tranquility was broken by a helicopter approaching them and then hovering for a minute. They both had the same thought...Califano.

On the morning in question, Califano told me he had just had a call from President Jimmy Carter, who had been in office only a few weeks. Carter was touring the various government agencies to say hello to the workers and get input, the only President to do so of the four I experienced. Apparently, a woman who worked in the Department of Agriculture had expressed her concern that as a deaf person, she could not enjoy television and hear the breaking news, things that most Americans took for granted. She asked him if, as President, he could do something about it. He called Joe, Joe called me, and the process began.

Actually, the Secretary called me because he knew we were doing something related to television captioning already. A program called "Captioned Films for the Deaf" had begun as a federally funded lending library, signed into law by President Eisenhower in 1958. Over the years it had grown to just over $2 million and arrangements had been made with Hollywood to have open captions, or subtitles, added to its films. Through a contractor within the field of deafness, we at BEH lent these films out to organizations and schools that served deaf children and adults. Over the years, the legislation had been amended to support the development and distribution of other technology to schools and classes for children who were deaf, after the program had been transferred to BEH.

We were also supporting an effort at a media center in Tennessee to develop a practical approach to captioning television and had held a conference in Knoxville, at which a number of broadcasters and other experts discussed the idea. In addition, we had made a grant to WGBH in Boston, a public broadcasting station, to caption a few of their programs.

WGBH found that a number of viewers did not like the visible, "open," captions at the bottom of the television screen, finding them distracting. Since no station wants to drive viewers away, WGBH came up with the idea of captioning only the second showing of a program, usually later in the week and at a later hour in the evening, after "primetime." One captioned program was "Masterpiece Theatre," which a substantial audience appreciated even if it was not "Mash" or "Mission Impossible." The other was the cooking program by the famous chef Julia Childs. Our informal polling suggested that a smaller group welcomed that program. One wag at our office said that at least the viewers who read captions did not have to listen to Ms. Child's legendary and somewhat distracting voice.

I began the quest to expand the program by visiting several leading producers and production companies, speaking with top officials of Norman Lear's "All in the Family;" Grant Tinker, who produced his then wife's "Mary Tyler Moore Show," and Lew Wasserman who headed MCA and was a friend of Secretary Califano.

They all told me that the upfront costs and time involved in captioning was too much to expect from them. They had very tight deadlines for turning shows over to the networks, and their main earnings came later in the process when syndication and overseas contracts were arranged. They also mentioned the need to work with the Screen Writers Guild, as any captioning that changed wording would need its approval. Further, they said that no matter what they agreed to do if the networks, did not want to show a captioned product, the networks had the final say. All offered cooperation, as did the Screen Writers, if things could be worked out. Clearly, the networks were going to be the key players.[8]

While gathering this information, we contracted with the Public Broadcasting Service (PBS) to develop a process of "closed captioning" that would be invisible to viewers. If they wished to see the captions, they could do so by using a special decoder. At the time there were no encoding or decoding devices, but broadcasters were familiar with an attempt by the National Bureau of Standards to send time signals using "line 21," which is part of the blank space under the transmitted picture. If you have ever had your picture roll up or down the screen you may have

8 The visit to Hollywood opened other, unexpected doors. We continued to work with Norman Lear and his company, for example, which led, among other things, to a wonderful episode of "All in the Family" in which Archie Bunker atttempted to plane a door and a neighbor kid with Down Syndrome noticed and rightly corrected his mistakes.

noticed a black space between the video frames. That "vertical blanking element" contains line 21 and other data channels that can be used to transmit information.

PBS and its chief engineer at the time, John Ball, began to work on the technology for prototype testing with BEH paying the costs through a series of large grants, totaling more than $1 million over several years.

Visiting NBC

I made appointments with the three national networks, ABC, NBC and CBS, to speak with them about the possibility of airing captioned programming. My first meeting was at the Washington headquarters of NBC. I brought along Mac Norwood, the head of our Captioned Films and Media Branch. Norwood had become deaf around age five, probably as a result of a virus or bacteria that caused a high fever. Because he had already developed language skills by then, Norwood's speech was quite intelligible, although its tonal qualities marked him as a person who could not hear (he used sign language with other people who were deaf). With his early language and speech foundation, Norwood had been able to excel at school and had successfully completed graduate work in the areas of technology and deafness.

While Norwood was an excellent speech reader (often called lip-reading), he used an interpreter, Ginny Lewis, to be sure he did not miss anything in business conversations. (We worked with the Civil Service Commission to create a position as "interpreter" that also encompassed administrative assistant duties.) Lewis was the daughter of deaf parents, as are many of the best sign language translators. Speech reading is a skill that relies on the reader's familiarity with language as well as the outer movements of the mouth while making sounds. The context of the discussion helps the reader predict what word might be next. People with hearing can make excellent lip readers if they practice the skill. Many older people do so, without even being aware of it, as their hearing declines.

I expected to meet someone in charge of programming at NBC, but when we entered the conference room, we were met by two attorneys. I knew at that point that we were not going to have a substantive discussion and events proved me right. The attorneys told us that NBC had no interest in captioning programs on its network. Further, one of them said that captions were unnecessary. He pulled from his pocket a cheap earplug attachment, similar to the ones that come with pocket radios, and threw it on the table. "Here, this is all you need," he insisted. "My mother-in-law is deaf, and we bought one of these which we plug into the TV and she gets everything. It only costs a couple of dollars." I tried to explain that our target audience consisted of people who had no, or very little, usable hearing, and would not benefit even from the powerful amplification. Norwood, Lewis and I left, shaking our heads, but there was worse to come.

Meeting with CBS

Our appointment at CBS headquarters in New York City was with Eugene Mater, assistant to the chairman, William Paley. We took the elevator to the top of the 38-story skyscraper known as Black Rock, designed by the famed Finnish architect Eero Saarinen. We were ushered into the luxurious executive floor and Mater's large office, with its spectacular view of the Manhattan skyline.

CBS had been working on a system called "Teletext" which was in use in a comparable form in England. The viewer could select to receive text messages on the TV screen. It had not been commercially successful in England and there were considerable technical problems with using it for captioning in the United States.

Our PBS engineers had advised us Teletext was at least five years away from commercial use and might never prove feasible. CBS was looking to operate the system on a fee basis, while our goal was free distribution of captions to the deaf and hearing impaired, just as the networks provided free programming to the general population.

We anticipated Mater raising the Teletext issue, but he surprised us by starting off citing the First Amendment to the Constitution, and declaring that CBS was unalterably opposed to captioning because it might require, in some instances, minor changes in the wording of the spoken language to keep up with the dialogue. We had considerable experience with films and with the PBS programming and no one, including the Screen Writers Guild, had raised any objections, but Mater insisted that CBS would defend the Constitution vigorously and oppose any attempts to change even a word of dialogue.

I mentioned the use of verbatim captioning, which could be done on virtually all pre-recorded programs (as most primetime programs then were). We could avoid situations that might present a problem and we would have someone, a contractor or CBS itself, do the captioning so they could exercise control. Mater was not impressed. He raised the issue of cost, saying CBS could not justify the expense, given the small number of people who were deaf. I replied that assuming Congress approved, and I felt that was likely, we would pay the costs and asked if that would change their position. Mater sneered, "We don't want any federal money. The next thing you know we will have to follow Title this and Title that." The only possible interpretation of that statement was that it referred to the parts of the Civil Rights Acts which prohibited discrimination against minorities and women. That guess on my part proved correct as Mater followed up by saying, "CBS is not interested in minority group programming."

Somewhat dumbfounded, I replied that we were not speaking of special programming, just captioning the usual CBS programming. Mater's patience was coming to an end. As he rose from his chair to end the meeting, he said again, "CBS is not interested in minority group programming. We are not interested in programming for the Chinese, the Mexicans, for the deaf, or what have you."

Norwood, who carefully followed the dialogue with Lewis' sign language translation could not believe his eyes. He looked to me with an expression that conveyed, "Did he really say that?" I nodded in the affirmative and we left. Hurtling down the express elevator to street level, I had the feeling we had been visiting a very foreign place with completely different values from the real world. In shock, we went across the street to Toots Shor's Restaurant and had a drink, although it was only 11:30 in the morning and it was not our custom to consume liquor, even at a more reasonable lunchtime.

Breakthrough with ABC

We met in Washington with Julius "Julie" Barnathon and Leonard Matkin from ABC. Barnathon was the head of ABC's engineering. Later, he held the title of President of Engineering and Operations. He was the guy who Roone Arledge, the widely renowned president of ABC Sports and later head of the network's operations, took out to remote sites for "Wide World of Sports," or for the Olympics, and said, "Julie, make it happen." And Barnathon did, to great praise. He had attended one of our conferences on captioning at the Tennessee center and seemed interested, at least in theory. Matkin was on the programming and policy side and while he deferred to Barnathon during our conversations, it was clear he had a different attitude than the NBC and CBS representatives.

As we talked, Barnathon mentioned a number of problems that he felt had to be solved if captioning television was going to be given serious consideration. He did not rule it out, though, and even said ABC would cooperate with the engineering problems and might work with PBS on the encoding and decoding process. After a discussion of our objectives and some of his questions, he said he would write to me and send me a list of the obstacles that needed to be overcome. We left, very grateful for the positive attitude, which may have been influenced by the views of Leonard Goldenson, the chairman of ABC, who had a daughter with cerebral palsy and was active in support of the United Cerebral Palsy Association.

When Barnathon's letter arrived and we checked with PBS, it seemed as though all the conditions could be met. Essentially, the system had to be designed so it would not interfere with the ABC signal. ABC engineers would cooperate to make that happen. There also needed to be a non-profit captioning entity, so that if ABC went ahead based on a certain cost for captions, the supplier would not suddenly "jack up" the price, leaving the network with the option of paying or cutting off the service and having to endure the subsequent outrage of the population of deaf people. The other technical issues were of less significance, and there was a bonus: ABC would be willing to pay a share of captioning costs for its programming.

It was a huge breakthrough. With one network willing to move ahead, the others would have to fall in line eventually. Now the task was to make ABC's participation in the program possible.

Developing a Decoder

PBS engineering, led by John Ball, developed an encoder over several years using approximately $1 million of BEH support funds. The encoder took the television signal and converted it into electronic markers on Line 21, invisible on a normal TV set. It was a big piece of equipment for television engineering studios. The decoder, however, had to be small enough to fit easily on top of a television set, or near it. It also had to be reasonably enough priced so that ordinary people who were deaf would be able to afford it.

When we began to speak to equipment manufacturers, with PBS's help, no one was interested. They considered a device for people who were deaf "a thin market" because only relatively few of them, perhaps several hundred thousand, would purchase such equipment. While some sources quoted millions of persons who were deaf, the numbers were based on studies of hearing loss, usually for medical reasons, not people who would actually require or wish to have captioning.

For a fee, PBS enlisted one of its board members, an attorney named Michael Curzon, from the powerhouse Washington law firm, Arnold & Porter. The firm did a great deal of work related to the Federal Communications Commission (FCC), which ultimately would have to approve the use of Line 21 for captioning.

In Washington circles, Arnold & Porter was perhaps best known as the firm that Abe Fortas had been with before being appointed to the Supreme Court. It also happened to be the firm where Joseph A. Califano had practiced before becoming HEW Secretary. At the time, his reported $500,000 separation fee from the firm was considered scandalously high by some, although with CEOs making tens, even hundreds of millions today, and baseball player Alex Rodriguez getting paid $250 million over 10 years, it now seems like "chump change."

Califano's tie with the firm became an issue later on. When he found that Mike Curzon was working on the project and being indirectly paid by BEH/HEW funds through the PBS contract, he "exploded." Apparently, he was unhappy because someone might think he played a role in getting Arnold & Porter an account, which in fact was not the case.

One of HEW's top attorneys, Richard I. Beattie, who served as associate general counsel and as general counsel, reviewed the situation carefully and calmed the Secretary down. Beattie, a brilliant and affable man, also helped throughout the project by having a staff attorney reporting to him carefully review the legal issues of dealing with PBS, ABC and various electronic firms. Later, when the project was questioned by contracting and grants personnel unused to HEW dealing with for-profit companies, the meticulous legal review that Dick and his associates had done quickly put that issue to rest. (For more on Beattie's role in the government and private sector, see part IV, Chapter 15.)

Mike Curzon turned out to be the key player in making the deals that were necessary for the caption project to succeed. Through Arnold & Porter, he had access to high levels of companies like Sears, Texas Instruments and others. He also was closely involved with major insurance companies that, surprisingly, turned out to have a critical role.

Texas Instruments, after on and off again negotiations, agreed to make a "chip" which would be the brains for the decoder, but wanted a $1 million minimum order. We knew that it would be almost impossible for the OE contract and grant bureaucrats to approve such a deal, given their unfamiliarity with dealing with profit-making companies. Sears considered offering the decoders through its catalogue and perhaps in its stores. Conversations with its affiliate, Sanyo, the Japanese electronics manufacturer, which made many Sears products, were cumbersome, and months went by with negotiations and considerations that seemed to go nowhere.

Meanwhile, Curzon came up with a strategy in which an insurance company would guarantee the $1 million to be repaid if and when sales from the decoder would reach that figure. While Curzon did not say so, I am sure he talked the company into taking that risk as a charitable act, should the project not succeed and pay off.

As things finally fell into place on the decoder side, we followed ABC's recommendation and set up a new non-profit entity called the National Captioning Institute (NCI). The organization was to be housed in Washington and headed by John Ball, who would leave PBS to be its president.

Originally I had thought we might involve a university in New York, probably Columbia Teachers College at Columbia University, which had a very strong special education program that included training teachers for the deaf. Another possibility was NYU, which was building a strong mass communications program. After ABC considered the possibility, it decided against it, wanting an organization dedicated to captioning and believing that a university would have other, bigger "fish to fry." ABC had a lot at stake. It was starting up something that people who were deaf were desperately seeking, and it did not want to get into a situation where those hopes would be destroyed and ABC would be blamed.

After NCI was established, PBS agreed to give the new non-profit the encoding equipment needed. At the same time, BEH agreed to a grant to produce a certain number of hours of captioned programming to be identified by ABC and PBS. We also had the option to purchase special programming, such as children's shows and sporting events, by paying the captioning costs.

In typical free market tradition, it only took a few years before several private, for-profit captioning firms sprung up, and along with WGBH in

Boston, became competitors of NCI. As is often the case, NCI had the burden of supporting the research and development that led to "live time captioning" and later the start-up costs for chips being inserted in all new television sets with screens larger than 13 inches. The small spin-offs, often headed by former NCI employees, had no such costs and could undercut NCI pricing.

People who were deaf rejoiced when captioning began. It was an enormous breakthrough for them, not just in entertainment, but in education as well. Television stations, newly aware of the audience of deaf and hearing impaired people, began to run open captions of emergency events like tornadoes and earthquakes. One of the best arguments before Congress in support of the captioning project came to us from a deaf person in Los Angeles. When an earthquake hit, all the information available to her was in the form of audio on television and radio. She had to wait until the next morning to read about it in the newspaper, not much help during the emergency, when detailed evacuation procedures and other news was critical.

FCC Approval and Revisiting Gene Mater

When all the pieces were in place, the last step was to get approval from the FCC. A hearing was scheduled and, not surprisingly, Gene Mater and CBS were going to attend to oppose granting approval.

Through a twist of fate, the documentary news program "CBS Reports" and its well-known reporter, Marlene Saunders, interviewed me about PL 94-142 and the growing "disability movement" a few weeks before the hearings. At one point Saunders asked me if there actually were people who opposed these gains or resisted helping the disabled. I gave her some examples and mentioned that CBS was resisting captioning, recounting my conversation with Gene Mater and his statement, "CBS is not interested in minority group programming." I hoped she would not be offended by my frankness. Far from being offended by me, she was offended by CBS's corporate policy, and reported on the air that her parent company, according to Gene Mater, had such a policy.

Before the hearings were held, I went to see FCC Commissioner Tyrone White, told him the story and arranged for him to see the "CBS Reports" segment.

During the hearings, Mater testified against captioning, mentioning CBS's better alternative (which never materialized, by the way). When Commissioner White asked him if CBS had a "not interested in minority group programming" policy, Mater said "no." White then showed the clip from "CBS Reports." Mater mumbled something about CBS news being a law unto itself and not necessarily informed on corporate policy, and slunk off into a corner, metaphorically. Norwood, Lewis and I considered it poetic justice well served.

With PL 94-142, the Education for All Handicapped Children Act, creating a historic opportunity to provide special education to millions of children with disabilities, the arrival of captioned television was lost in the shuffle, but it was enormously rewarding for the people involved in making it happen and to the population who would benefit from it. That group, interestingly, turned out to include many immigrants from Korea, Japan, China and elsewhere who found they could learn English more easily watching and listening at the same time. More decoders were eventually sold on the West Coast for second language learning than for people who were deaf. Research BEH supported through NCI also found that watching captioned television was useful for learning to read, including teaching reading to children with learning disabilities.

At the end of his term as HEW Secretary, Joe Califano told me that of all the momentous activities of the department, he took particular pleasure in our having made captioning available to persons who were deaf. I did, too.

Summary

During the period after its creation, BEH and the federal programs supporting education for children with special educational needs became a significant part of federal education aid. From its small beginnings, the creation of programs like early childhood programs, centers for children who were deaf and blind, and the gathering of them all together in the Education of the Handicapped Act—what is called an "omnibus" in Congress—established a permanent federal role. Further, its status in OE made the Bureau a major participant in the budget and policy discussions that led to establishing federal priorities. Pushed internally by the BEH and externally by Congress on behalf of parents and school systems that wished to provide programs, federal policy makers in HEW and in the President's OMB had to carefully consider issues affecting the nature and extent of federal aid.

An important message for people who wish to affect public policy is that one should be willing to approach a desired goal with small steps taking what can be approved, supporting important constituencies, and building relationships with key "Hill" staffers. Writing letters or emails is not the path to successful legislation. Personal contact and pointing out the deep involvement of people "back home" is the way to institute permanent change.

PART THREE

Launching a Campaign to Educate Every Handicapped Child by 1980

As the nation experiences education under the recent emphasis on testing, including testing of children's performance to evaluate teachers and schools, there are those who see hope for progress and laud the benefits from additional expenditures on reading and measurement of achievement. Others worry that special education and programs for children with disabilities may be harmed by the emphasis on group testing of elementary school children. They point to reports of these children being grouped in a way that removes their scores from those of children without disabilities in order to keep the school's average scores higher.

The jury is out on whether or not the new support for, and emphasis on, reading will resolve the problems of many children now seen as needing special education and so "reform" education. The experience with the development of federal policy and programs for students with disabilities demonstrates that major government programs do not succeed overnight. In 1967, when the Carey Bill, the first Education of Handicapped Children Act, was signed into law and Congress passed the initial appropriations, only $2.5 million were distributed to the states to begin the program. Recently, four decades later, revisions and extensions of this act provide over $12 billion annually to the states. Yet no one is arguing that the educational problems of children with disabilities have been adequately served. (To put these figures in perspective, $12 billion represents only about 15% of total special education expenditures.)

If there is a lesson, it is that major federal policy generally takes many years to evolve—Social Security and Medicare took decades and are still in process. For a program to have a comprehensive effect there must be a massive and complex plan. It is difficult to grasp all the parameters of such a challenge. The general governmental response, whether at a federal, state or local level, is to aim at a problem, apply a limited amount of resources, and hope some significant good will be accomplished. With millions of teachers, tens of thousands of school districts and tens of millions of children, the task of "changing" education represents an almost incomprehensible challenge.

In this part we will look at legislation that was designed to effect such a major change in American education—to erase years of inequity faced by children with special educational needs. Not content to merely improve the opportunities for special education, it was an ambitious attempt to create a new process of educational treatment, a new set of responsibilities for the schools, and a fundamental change in the "civil rights" of children with disabilities and their families.

CHAPTER 9

"Education for All"

We at BEH did not originate the concept of "education for all." In 1970, there were already activities designed to achieve that end on a state level. I traveled to Washington State, for example, to meet with parents and professionals and appear on Seattle television in order to help publicize their efforts, as well as those of key local legislators.

Norris Haring and Alice Hayden, professors at the Experimental Education Unit of the University of Washington, were working closely with parents and state legislator Marjorie Lynch, (later Undersecretary of HEW in the Nixon Administration in Washington). There were similar thrusts in several other states, including Massachusetts and Michigan, not always under the banner of "education for all," but aiming at the same goal.

In Washington, D.C., the budget and policy people on the "Transition Team" for the new Nixon Administration in 1969 rebuffed our efforts, but we were encouraged by Commissioner Sidney Marland's willingness to help us promote the concept of "Education for All Handicapped Children by 1980." Notwithstanding limited federal financial assistance, we began to plot a course of action. One part of that strategy was to use our best efforts to present planning and budget documents to the HEW and OMB, detailing the special education needs in rational rather than emotional terms, since "budgeteers" pride themselves on hard-nosed, objective analysis.

A "Catalytic" Strategy

We proposed modifying the administration of the current government special education programs as part of a "capacity building" and "catalytic" strategy. Washington loves acronyms and special terminology, so we chose "capacity" and "catalytic" because they suggested the potential for big changes from relatively small precipitating origins. For example, we argued that our federal grants to colleges and universities for teacher education accomplished much more than just support for a limited number of students. We had restructured those grants from the traditional arrangement in which a college received, for example, $5,000 and gave $2,500 to a student for tuition and kept $2,500 for expenses. In the new arrangement, a grant was given to an "Institution of Higher Education" (IHE) in response to a proposal that the training funds would increase the capacity of the IHE to provide training to more people or to train people for an unmet need. Examples might include hiring a new faculty member with the funds or giving a number of smaller grants to more students. Or a university might start a program in an area like "learning disabilities" or "severely handicapped," where there was a great need for teachers and little capacity.

We also argued that colleges and universities, encouraged by federal grants and with growing student enrollments, would add funding of their own to special education programs. There was evidence that IHEs were creating departments of special education and expanding them as a result of the "catalytic" effect of federal grants. We compared our calculated grant strategies with other federal spending patterns, which were derisively called "stump money" in "budget circles." That referred to putting federal funds on a metaphoric "stump" and letting the recipients come get them with no strings attached. Conversely, there were advocates for just that process, particularly Republicans, who felt that "block grants" (stump) with no strings attached gave needed flexibility to state or local officials. The battle between "categorical" ("targeted") and "block" funding persists today.

The "catalytic" arguments could be made for our other model project authorities and our research and demonstration efforts. We funded programs to demonstrate effective practices or to develop new ones. These programs resulted in replicated programs that could be and were supported with local funds. In our grant announcements we emphasized that replication of successful demonstration projects should be a part of the submitted proposal. Other examples of a catalytic effect might include new personnel being trained in areas where shortages existed, such as early childhood or the severely disabled. In fact, new journal articles and books, and the new research base which was being formed all had a major impact.

One example that pleased us grew out of an early childhood grant we awarded to Professor Peggy Wood of the University of Georgia to serve children with emotional and behavioral disorders, "The Rutland Project." The wife of the Governor of Georgia came to visit the project and was very impressed. Soon her husband, the Governor, agreed to replicate the project at about a dozen mental health centers around the state. Peggy called me, overjoyed by the replications and after I congratulated her, I asked, "Peggy, I'm sorry, but who is the Governor now?" "Why," she answered with her southern drawl, "Jimmy Carter."

Bob Herman

One of the key players in these strategy formulations was Robert B. Herman. I had discovered him in our small, two-person planning office, which was turning out good work. During a period of time when the "planning officer" was away, Herman had filled in at our meetings, and it quickly became apparent as he presented ideas that he had a lively, incisive mind. His training as an economist and systems analyst complemented our disability-related information. As he presented his thoughts, I realized that he must have been generating many of the good plans and strategies that had issued from that office.

Herman is an example of the "great American dream." He was born in the Bronx, "in the shadow of Yankee Stadium," as he liked to say, repeating a classic New York cliché. He had attended Bronx Science High School which, although public, was available only to the best and brightest students who had to compete for entry. He went on to the City College of New York (CCNY), which was tuition free at that time, and a very fine school. Its Economics department was among the nation's best. Weaving his career around two military stints—he was a "reservist" called up again to serve as a tank commander in Korea after serving in the post-WWII Army—he began working in the Labor Department.

As an economist at the Department of Labor, Herman had been involved in implementing a forward-looking program originated by Sar Levitan, a well- respected professor at Johns Hopkins University, known for his analysis of social policy and influence on government programs. It was part of a "New Careers" strategy, to lift people out of poverty by structuring employment programs so that untrained people could progress into leadership positions by learning on the job. The "career ladder" concept, where opportunities for climbing were designed into jobs filled by entry-level workers, was a key ingredient in Labor's programs to implement President Johnson's "War on Poverty."

Herman used his quick thinking and facility in "economic-speak" to help us put our special education goals into language that the budget analysts would consider rational, and not the "bleeding heart" stuff they expected from people running the programs for the disabled or economically disadvantaged. I quickly promoted him to head of planning (there was an appropriate position elsewhere for his predecessor, trained in special education). When the time came for me to select a deputy, Herman became the number two person in BEH, with the official title of Deputy Associate Commissioner and Deputy Director. Later, when President Carter nominated me to serve as Assistant Secretary for Special Education and Rehabilitative Services in the brand new Department of Education, I selected Herman to be Deputy Assistant Secretary.

No one, inside or outside government, worked harder, put in longer hours, or advocated more effectively for children with disabilities. His commitment to children did not weaken his instincts as an economist or budget analyst. He held us to a high standard and won us respect from the planners and budgeteers we had to convince.

***

An example of the impact of his training and style of thinking came in a family story. Once, Herman was playing Monopoly with his young son, Andrew. Noticing that Andrew wasn't purchasing more properties, he asked why; ten-year-old Andrew replied in the language of an economist, "I have a cash-flow problem."

Another example, perhaps harking back to his tank commander days, came when the Office of Education (OE) and the General Services Administration (GSA), which deals with federal office space and many of the operational logistics of government, decided to move BEH to a building that had to be entered by climbing a flight of granite steps. As a bureau serving and employing people with disabilities—a model for other agencies—we did not want to be in a non-wheelchair-accessible building.

OE and GSA pointed out that a person in a wheelchair could go down the ramp into the garage and use the elevator there. They neglected to mention that the route passed through an odiferous area where garbage from the café and elsewhere was stored, or that the idea of visitors having to go through the garage at all was unappealing.

When my logical arguments produced no results, I essentially refused to move until a ramp was built to the front entrance. The government functionaries enforcing the terms of the "Architectural Compliance Board"—ironically, I served on that board—said that would be too expensive. In response, we ignored the written orders they sent: We did not pack up any of our things; we just kept working. Finally, I was summoned to the head office to receive the orders in person. I sent Bob Herman.

When he returned he told us that they had decided to build the ramp. I asked how he had accomplished that, and without cracking a smile, he related how he told them we would move, and there would be representatives from the *Washington Post* and the television channels present to watch the event transpire. He wasn't a tank commander by accident.

***

To maximize our arguments that the federal funds could have a "multiplier effect," Herman suggested a strategy of recruiting the states to use the funds from our grant programs more effectively. Since they had virtually total authority on how to spend the money, any cooperative effort would have to be made willingly on their part. To recruit them into a joint effort, we organized a program called "mutuality of planning" and held a series of conferences which presented planning concepts and strategies to state special education directors and their key staff.

A number of states agreed with our rationale that the OMB and Congress would look more favorably on the program if the states spent federal funds on high-priority activities. This would contrast with the practice of simply distributing funds to the local schools which might use them to support existing programs with no growth or innovation.

While the federal law included a proviso that states had to use federal funds to "supplement not supplant" local funds, there were ways to get around it. While a state could not lawfully reduce the amount it was spending on special education, it could, for example, leave its funding at the same level and use the federal funds to increase the program, thereby avoiding having to spend more of its own funds to meet its commitments to its children.

That did occur in some instances, but the overall impact on children served was limited; with the federal law paying only a small share of total costs, the rapidly growing demand for special education resulted in states and "locals" having to increase their budgets.

Examples of the effect of "mutuality of planning" included states starting new programs for children who were underserved. For example, there were few local and state programs for children with multiple and severe handicaps, and few states had funded early childhood education programs. The federal demonstration programs created an interest by parents and special education teachers, a case of supply causing demand. Special programs to train teachers in these new areas were also funded, first by federal funds. In most states these programs served as models creating demand for state-funded replications.

While there were a number of states that provided good examples for us to use in budget hearings, Florida, with Wendy Cullar as the planning officer, did a particularly good job (she later served as head of the U.S. Office of Special Education). Cullar embraced the "mutuality of planning" concept of working cooperatively with BEH. Rather than just distributing the federal funds to the local schools, she targeted the resources to increase needed services and encouraged local funding for these programs so that the following year's federal funds could further expand services.

Expanded Demonstration Strategy

Building on the growing acceptance by Department and Office of Management and Budget (OMB) analysts as well as Congress of our activist lines of attack, we began to talk about expanding the "catalytic" strategy into an "expanded demonstration model." Essentially, we proposed that larger grants from the federal government would provide a critical mass in the states, raising both the visibility and demand for programs. This was in part an example of words of art—since the Nixon OMB did not want to support federal funds for broad-scale service programs, we created a rationale for increases in federal funding, calling it something else.

In other words, a significant federal grant would result in much greater state and local effort. We hoped to increase the federal share quickly from about $50 million to $250 or $300 million, but although our logical approach received kudus, the Nixon Administration's budget office remained unforthcoming. It was frustrating, but as mentioned earlier, we had a philosophy of coming back to play another day. As the Chinese saying goes, "A Journey of 1000 miles begins with a single step."

Aiming at State Legislation

With major federal aid for local special education programs not on the immediate horizon, we decided to begin a new approach to gaining support and increasing pressure for additional services for children.

We worked closely with the Council for Exceptional Children (CEC) in Arlington, Virginia, on legislative proposals going back to my work on the Carey Committee. Fred Weintraub had become that non-profit organization's governmental relations specialist—read lobbyist. Weintraub was ABD (all but dissertation) in Special Education from Teachers College, Columbia University and had classroom experience, so he was well suited for his job. He was bright, aggressive in a positive way, and had what might today be called a "New York edge." Fred, as Bill Geer before him, had education for children with disabilities as his single-minded focus. CEC was much to be commended in my mind; it represented teachers as a professional group, but did not promote teachers' benefits, other than having the classroom resources they needed to help children.

In spring 2012 Fred was honored as a Pioneer of CEC and I was asked to contribute a bit about him for a presentation at the CEC's convention in Denver. I mentioned that he had a propensity for wearing cowboy hats at one point in the early 70s, and that I felt he probably was a role model for the character Billy Crystal played in "City Slickers." That brought chuckles from the audience at the time.

He and I had worked together to try to persuade the incoming Nixon "Transition Team" to make education for handicapped children a priority. Shortly after an election, the incoming Administration puts together a number of what are known as transition teams—groups of advisors and future Administration workers chosen from among their supporters to review federal programs and make recommendations about them. Although the education team included John Melcher, the state director of special education in Wisconsin, who supported our goal of increased funding, our efforts were not successful in creating a priority for the new Administration.

Weintraub and his colleague, Alan Abeson, felt an ongoing policy center at CEC would be helpful for generating state and federal legislation. He and Bob Herman worked out many of the details, and the program for such a center was ultimately submitted, looked at by field reviewers for BEH and recommended for funding.

CEC's policy center played a significant role in creating additional special educational opportunity in the early 1970s and became another example of how we attempted to use federal funds to strengthen the leadership potential of special educators in "the field." Helping to boost organizations of teachers, parents and administrators became a basic strategy of our effort to provide "Education for All Handicapped Children."

The Education Commission of the States and the Model State Plan

The policy center developed a "Model State Plan," which attracted some attention from special education professionals, but was generally ignored by general education policy makers. I decided to approach a Denver-based organization called "The Education Commission of the States" (ECS), which had been formed in part to counter what its leaders felt was an overwhelming presence by the federal government with its new education laws and requirements. CEC was also working with ECS in several states to adopt the Model Statute.

ECS's delegations were appointed by the Governors of each state, who made sure that the makeup included other policy makers, primarily legislators and state board of education members. The Governors were eager to develop a unified presentation of what they felt were the education needs of the states while concurrently influencing distribution patterns of federal funds so their impact would be more productive and less intrusive.

We met with ECS staff members to speak with them about our goal of "Education for All Handicapped Children by 1980" and to solicit their support. They invited me to address their national conference in Boston in an attempt to enlist their state constituents in "The Education for All" movement.

One concept that won favor was for us to support a series of regional conferences sponsored by ECS and involving CEC, in which delegations from each state would have a chance to study the CEC "Model Statute" with CEC staff as presenters. Several legislators in ECS, already enthusiastic about expanding special education in their states, sponsored a resolution supporting the 1980 goal, and ECS was the first major educational organization besides CEC to adopt the goal.

With the help of a grant of $300,000 to $400,000 from BEH, a series of conferences took place in various regions of the United States which employed CEC's model state plan. We shared general information about the plan and participated in discussions by the entire group. Then each delegation met separately to confer about adopting the plan for its particular state.

As a result of that effort, in conjunction with CEC, we were able to stimulate local growth in virtually every state, modifying and strengthening legislation for disabled children over the next few years.

We were pleased. It was one of the most successful intervention strategies we launched that grew out of federal planning and funding, and it represented a major step toward "education for every handicapped child."

CHAPTER 10

The Courts

Parallel to our efforts, a significant public policy force was developing in 1971-72. Parents, frustrated by the lack of state laws requiring schools to educate their disabled children—or, if they were on the books, received scant or limited enforcement—turned to the courts.

PARC Makes its Case

The Public Interest Law Center of Philadelphia (PILCOP) had decided to represent the Pennsylvania Association for Retarded Children (PARC) in challenging the Education Department of Pennsylvania and the laws and practices which allowed schools to exclude children with mental retardation from educational programs. As mentioned earlier, no state included all of its children with handicaps in educational programs. Those with more than mild to moderate, so-called "educable" mental retardation could, at best, find themselves in "state schools for the mentally retarded." It was widely understood that most of these programs were substandard and some, as later court cases demonstrated, atrocious.

Tom Gilhool was the lead attorney who brought the case in federal district court. The Pennsylvania Secretary of Education was the named defendant on behalf of the department and the state laws it administered. The case and the ultimate decision became popularly known as the PARC case. (In an ironic turn, years later Gilhool became Secretary of Education in Pennsylvania and sometimes found himself on the other side of the law he helped to bring about.)

The CEC policy center offered assistance to Gilhool and helped identify a number of prominent special educators who would testify against the state's position. We at BEH also suggested witnesses. As the case progressed it became apparent that the plaintiffs were going to prevail and Pennsylvania decided to agree to a "consent order." Under such an order the litigation ceases and the defendants and plaintiffs agree to a settlement before the judge's decision that remedies the situation under dispute.

PARC was a major breakthrough, the first special education legal case to challenge the status quo. It followed by example, if not precise legal precedent, the Wyatt v. Stickney case, which had challenged conditions in a state mental hospital in Alabama. The case was decided for the plaintiffs by federal judge Frank Johnson, who was also a trailblazer in Civil Rights cases and occupied the top spot on Governor George Wallace's "enemies list."

Frank Johnson was born in the hill country of Alabama, not the historic home of plantations. He was a Republican, not unusual in that area, and a graduate of the University of Alabama law school. He was appointed by President Eisenhower as a U.S. Attorney and then as a Federal District Judge.

Judge Johnson's decision set standards of care for the mental hospital and was known as a "Right to Treatment" case. It had a major effect on later proceedings in other federal district courts and on the emerging "Right to Education" cases, as they were called.

When the PARC case was settled by "consent decree" in 1971, the primary stipulation was that Pennsylvania agreed to stop excluding children with mental retardation who needed special education in local or state programs. But there were other significant provisos as well, and they became precedents for the federal law that emerged the following year and would be considered by Congress in the period from 1972 to 1975. These stipulations included parental rights to be informed and involved in decisions about their children's education, and the concept of children being placed in "the least restrictive" environment appropriate to their needs. They were part of the PARC agreement and later became part of the federal law. PARC and its advocates made the first giant step under court-ordered federal law that led to significant change for all of America's children with disabilities.

Mills v. Board of Education

In 1972, another federal case had a critical impact on the rights for children with disabilities movement. Mills v. Board of Education, usually referred to simply as "Mills," was heard in the District of Columbia. A non-profit group based in the District, the Mental Health Law Project, represented the plaintiffs and won a verdict that extended the protections of PARC to all children with all disabilities, not just the mentally retarded.

We in BEH took particular delight in the judge having ruled that failure to have sufficient funds was not a suitable excuse for not offering special education. It answered a refrain we had heard ad nauseam from local, state and federal officials for years. The judge said, in essence, that no government ever has enough funds to implement everything it chooses to do or provide for everything a society needs. What it must do is assure that the insufficient funding does not fall most heavily and in a discriminatory way on one class of citizens, in this case, children with disabilities. That finding took the wind out of the classic state denials of requests for more special education programming.

With the landmark decision of PARC and Mills, the dam broke and scores of cases were filed across the nation. This added further fuel to the new legislative efforts at state and local levels and the movement for the "Right to Education for Every Handicapped Child by 1980" really took off.

Testifying in Court

I received a call one day in 1973 from an attorney at the Mental Health Law Project telling me of an upcoming case in a Maryland State Court. The issues were essentially the same as those in the earlier federal cases—Maryland was being sued because it did not provide education to all of its children with disabilities, despite a provision in the state constitution that promised education to all children. The reason the attorney called me was that he had found out the State was going to use one of BEH's staff, Dr. Ed Sontag, to testify in its defense. The Mental Health Law Project, knowing of my leadership of the federal effort, was astonished that a Bureau professional would be on the opposite side of this issue.

I was surprised and disappointed, but I also recognized that there was a First Amendment right involved here. I felt it would be inappropriate to try to restrain Sontag from testifying, although OE attorneys said he could not speak as a representative of the agency, only as a private citizen of Maryland. Instead, I agreed to the attorney's request to testify for his side. I called Maryland State officials and explained that I felt Sontag's involvement left me no choice but to support my views and the goals of BEH.

This was the first time I had given testimony in a court of law. I was not concerned about the challenge since by then I had testified repeatedly to Congressional committees on the basic subject and had given more than 100 speeches to various groups about the need to assure education for every child.

The judge asked me a series of questions that were at the heart of the case. Maryland officials claimed that they did not have enough trained teachers and so could not implement special education for their children in need right away. They wanted to delay getting started until teachers were available, for an indefinite number of years. As I was a witness, I was not present for Sontag's testimony, but I understand he supported the state's argument that without trained personnel it should not be required to serve disabled children.

In response to the judge's request to comment on that position, I agreed that the lack of trained teachers presented a difficult problem. On the other hand, there was no assurance that the state would ever have enough trained teachers, or it might take many years to get to that point, all the while children were being denied their "Constitutional" right to education. I suggested, instead, that the judge require Maryland to begin a program of in-service training for teachers during the school year and in summer programs, and perhaps initiate special incentives for recruitment. In the meantime, the most qualified people they had could begin serving the children. I agreed this was not a perfect solution—children would be receiving education from less than fully qualified teachers—but, in fact, that was already the case in almost every state, including Maryland, where many teachers had partial or provisional certification in special education.

The judge decided for the plaintiffs—the parents and children—and ordered the state to implement a program of services and teacher training. It was the only time I was directly involved in such a case, although I returned to court in connection with my duties two more times in criminal matters.

Ed Sontag returned to his duties at the Bureau for some time, then left voluntarily to relocate to Wisconsin where he had several friends on the state university's faculty. Later, in the Reagan Administration, Sontag returned to the Department of Education, where he led an effort to weaken the PL 94-142 regulations, (see Chapter 15). Happily, it failed.

CHAPTER 11

The Origins of The Education For All Handicapped Children Act

One day in 1972, I received a call from Lisa Walker, a new staff member of the Senate Committee on Labor and Public Welfare, who worked for its chairman, Harrison Williams (Democrat, NJ). The committee had responsibility for writing legislation dealing with education as well as health, labor and other issues, and Walker had good news: The Senator wanted to sponsor legislation for children with disabilities and was considering establishing a subcommittee focused on disability as well.

A political scientist by training, Walker had been an intern on the staff of Representative John Brademas, who chaired the House Select Education Subcommittee, which had jurisdiction over special education and vocational rehabilitation, among other responsibilities. The counsel for that subcommittee was Jack Duncan, who had previously worked in the legislative office in the Rehabilitation Services Administration and who was familiar with many disability-related issues. After her internship Walker was hired by Senator Williams, and he took her up on the suggestion that special education would be an important issue for the committee to pursue.

Walker, a young woman I estimated to be in her 20s, was somewhat different than many of her peers on "the Hill," who seemed to be as attuned to the "dating game," possibly with members of Congress, as to the job at hand. More serious-minded, she struck me as someone who wanted to get a job done that would be helpful to people.

The Senate Subcommittee on the Handicapped

Walker's enthusiasm was infectious, and I got off the phone energized. It was very exciting for us to think about having the chairman of the key Senate authorizing committee and his staff as advocates for education for children with disabilities. Having a subcommittee focused on disability would also have great significance, a sign of the growing Congressional interest in special education programming and policy. It was a big step in moving special education legislation into the Congressional mainstream, even more significant than our earlier consolidation of bills into the Education of the Handicapped Act had been.

***

Not everyone was pleased. I got a call from Steve Wexler, counsel to Chairman Claiborne Pell's Education subcommittee to come see him. Pell and the committee had been very instrumental in the successful passage of the consolidated "Education of the Handicapped Act," and considered special education their bailiwick. When we met, Steve asked me, "Haven't we treated you—meaning BEH and the disability field—well?" They had, I acknowledged, but went on to say that I didn't think they would mind losing that bit of jurisdiction. Pell was keen on higher education—a program providing money to help students attend colleges and universities is now known as the "Pell Grants." Further, the elementary and secondary education programs were much larger and more significant politically, as were vocational education and a variety of other programs the committee oversaw.

At the time, I felt that Steve looked at me as an ingrate, but we moved on and I cannot recall any difficulties going forward. Committee jurisdictions are not lightly altered—people in power hate giving up control over anything they consider their turf—but in this case we got away with it and the Subcommittee on the Handicapped became a reality under the aegis of Labor and Public Welfare.

***

During the initial call with Lisa Walker, I remember her asking, "What kind of a bill should we develop?" I replied, kidding, "How about an appropriations bill?" While that was not really possible through Chairman Williams' committee—generating bills and approving funds for them happens in completely separate venues—I said it because we both knew that there was authority under the existing "Title VI" to make grants for up to $200 million a year. For that to be fulfilled, the money had to be appropriated. At the time, BEH's actual appropriations were under $50 million.

I believed it was critical to get more money so we could make an impact on state and local practice. Whatever bill developed should also increase the likelihood of higher funding. From our point of view, in an ideal world, the bill could have made funding mandatory, each year providing the sum necessary to educate all handicapped children. Programs like Medicare and Medicaid had such formulas at that time, but Congress was already greatly concerned that their requirements would grow out of control. Such an entitlement formula for a new special education law was not politically feasible, but it never hurts to dream.

Senator Randolph Chairs the Subcommittee

Before Chairman Williams could establish the Subcommittee on the Handicapped and preside, Senator Jennings Randolph (Democrat, WV) made a claim to become its chairman.

Randolph was actually the senior member on the full Labor and Public Welfare Committee, but he had left chairmanship to Williams. Instead, Randolph had opted to chair the Public Works Committee, a more powerful assignment. Public Works made grants to every state for roads, bridges, federal construction projects and more. Not only did a lot of those projects find their way into West Virginia, but Senators desiring such projects had to come to Randolph for assistance in many cases, which multiplied his power manifold.

It wasn't clear at first why Randolph wanted to be chair of the new subcommittee about to be formed. True, he had been interested in the past in legislation that affected people with disabilities, including sponsoring bills to provide assistance to coal miners with black lung disease. He also was the co-sponsor of the Randolph-Sheppard Vending Stand Act, which gave people who were blind the opportunity to set up vending stands for newspapers, snacks, etc. in federal buildings.

A more likely explanation is that it was the behind-the-scenes work of Jack Forsythe, who had been general counsel to the committee and who had worked with Randolph over a number of years. Forsythe was, by then, married to Patria Winalski, and working on her behalf. Although it can only be surmised, the ensuing events suggested that Jack called on Randolph or a colleague on his staff and suggested that the Senator, as the senior member and with a background in disability-related matters, should use his seniority to claim the subcommittee. Members of Congress do not take lightly the opportunity to have more staff, which a subcommittee would provide. Williams agreed to that arrangement and lo and behold, Pat Winalski, now Pat Forsythe, was named by Randolph to become the staff director of the subcommittee. She wasted no time in pushing for any legislation dealing with special education to be a "Randolph bill" and one she would create. This led to a conflict—typical of Washington's turf battles—with Lisa Walker over sponsorship of the proposed legislation.

I am not sure if the rivalry was due to personal jealousy or just a case of Pat wanting the power. She and Walker were of different generations and certainly had different professional abilities, but Pat was a skilled political fighter, and her husband, Jack, was a long-term inside professional who knew how to use the levers of power. Pat, essentially, felt she had staked-out the "handicapped turf" and was used to getting her way.

Turf Battles

Chairman Williams went ahead with plans for a bill, S. 6, "The Education for All Handicapped Children's Act," and Walker, with her position on his staff, was in a strong position to gain support for it from other members of the committee. Theoretically if push came to shove, Williams' bill should prevail, but things are seldom that simple in Washington, and many factors can influence how the committee votes on a given piece of legislation, including, for example, the power of a Senator like Randolph to use his influence in Public Works to provide "pork" for a member's state.

Pat Forsythe also began working on a bill, S. 396, which was an extension of the existing Education of the Handicapped Act with its primary aim of providing grants to the states. Her plan was to increase the authorizations in the act and get backing for increased appropriations, which would effectively eliminate much of the need and support for Williams' legislation. S. 396 would be a Randolph bill, approved by his subcommittee and virtually unstoppable at the full-committee level without entering into a full-fledged political war, which put Chairman Williams in the unseemly position of appearing to be fighting for personal reasons—i.e., his own bill.

Another wrinkle was the court decision in Maryland, mentioned earlier, which came into play because Maryland was under the gun to provide education for thousands of children with special education needs. As a result, Senator Charles "Mac" Mathias (Republican, MD) was encouraged to add an amendment to the appropriations bill for education in his committee. A progressive Republican, Mathias was open to procuring funds for special education, and he was well liked by Democrats backing such attempts; Pat saw this route as a way to achieve her goals.

The Mathias Amendment would add over $600 million to the special education grants to the states, taking most of the wind out of the sails of S. 6. What Williams' bill had going for it with professionals and parents were provisions for the protection of parents and disabled children. They had been included because of the long history of excluding such children from educational programs by unilaterally identifying them as disabled and placing them in classes that were not suited for them. In some cases, children were categorized as disabled on the basis of tests not in the language they spoke. These unsavory practices had been documented in federal lawsuits. While S. 6 and its companion, H.R. 70, included provisions for providing parents and children with civil-rights type safeguards and more; S. 396 did not.

I was only one of several people who got involved in this dispute. While I was naturally drawn toward any activity which would increase the funds available for children from about $50 million to almost $700 million, I also felt S. 6 was the correct and necessary model for federal legislation.

I had known Pat and Jack Forsythe since my first years in Washington and had considered them friends at the time. Jack introduced me to Carey, opening the way for my appointment as director of the ad hoc Subcommittee on the Handicapped. We socialized and through Jack I met many of the influential lobbyists that were part of the education scene. While the lobbyists, for the most part, had little or no direct bearing on my programs, they provided insight into other education struggles (and paid for dinner). Pat's efforts on behalf of deaf children had been positive for the most part, although, as I noted earlier, it was often difficult to work with her because she always had a personal agenda.

In time, our relationship frayed over a number of issues. One was that Pat had to have things her way to the point of sabotaging programs—even for children with disabilities—if she didn't. For example, she got Jack to block the inclusion of children with learning disabilities in the definition of "disability" for federal legislation when the Carey Bill was included as Title VI of the Elementary and Secondary Education Act. At this point in time, she was more interested in "her" bill being passed, and perhaps in "beating" Walker, than she was in the content of the legislation.

When reasoning with her became impossible, I took a different route. I spoke to Colby King, then the key staffer on this issue for Senator Mathias. King, now a columnist for the *Washington Post*, understood the impact on S. 6. He had no interest in crippling the legislation, although he still had a mission on behalf of his boss—to get money for Maryland.

Fred Weintraub of the Council for Exceptional Children (CEC) exerted considerable efforts to head off what he felt would be a catastrophe for the future of special education. He organized teachers in Maryland and elsewhere to speak with Mathias, King and other staffers. Parents groups in Maryland and elsewhere did the same. It was, in basketball terms, "a full court press."

A compromise emerged, and I think Fred and CEC played the major role in getting there, Mathias agreed to make his amendment a one-year increase and to support the passage of S. 6 so that the money would be folded into the future appropriations under that bill when it became law.

That naturally ended the prospects for S. 396 and essentially assured the success of S. 6 in the Senate. My relationship with the Forsythes was badly damaged, however. The earlier battle over inclusion of children with learning disabilities, which Pat had resisted, created an ongoing strain. Finally, the Forsythes attempted to interfere in a grant process, something they had not done with me previously, pushing a friend's application for The National Center for Media and Materials we were planning to fund. The Center grant went to a competing bidder, not their choice, but the Forsythes' inappropriate attempt to pressure me was the final straw for our relationship.

CHAPTER 12

Key Concepts of The Education for All Handicapped Children Act

Lisa Walker and I agreed to begin meeting and talking together after Lisa's call and before the Randolph subcommittee emerged. People who were essential to the bill's development in the Congress were Jack Duncan, John Brademas, who was a natural sponsor for a companion House bill, and Fred Weintraub of the Council for Exceptional Children.

Over the next few years this "iron triangle" group—Walker, Duncan, Weintraub and myself—provided much of the strategy and content of the legislation, although other Congressional staff members as well as Congressmen and Senators played important roles in developing certain parts of the bills. Representatives of other groups interested in disability or in education in general also impacted the bill's provisions, giving suggestions and "feedback" information about issues that were of critical importance to them. Ultimately, their most important role was rallying political support for its passage.

"Free, Appropriate, Public Education" (FAPE)

The key concept in the legislation as it began to develop was to try to guarantee that children would have the opportunity to receive special education and that schools would no longer be able to "exclude" them for reasons of disability.

At the time, every state was failing to educate all of its handicapped children who should be eligible for programs. Even though many states had "mandatory" laws that were supposed to require school districts to do so, these laws were ineffective. Some had exceptions for children judged "not able to benefit" by a local superintendent or school official. Others had exclusions for children with disabilities deemed to be "very severe," and therefore "uneducable." Still others were simply never enforced by the states, and so local districts continued to serve some children and not others.

We wanted to make sure that the "zero reject" concept became the basis of the law—states had to guarantee "Free, Appropriate, Public Education" (FAPE) for every child.

No Federal "Right to Education"

But getting there was not just a matter of writing a federal law simply requiring the states to educate the children. That would have been possible if the federal Constitution said that education was a fundamental right, or if the Constitution had made the federal government responsible for education. There is, however, no mention of education in the Constitution and, therefore, it is up to the states to determine how to provide it.

A number of states did mention a commitment to public education for all children in their constitutions, and so the educational programs which excluded children were unlawful under their constitutions. That was affirmed in a number of court cases in various states, as happened in Maryland.

With no federal "mandate" possible, the best approach seemed to be a quid pro quo—to devise provisions in a plan that the states had to submit to the federal government before the federal funds in the new program were released. This was an approach used in much federal legislation. The "state plan" would voluntarily promise FAPE and various programs and policies and, in exchange, the state would receive the government money.

To get that kind of agreement, we believed the formula in the law had to be powerful enough—financially and therefore, politically—to generate a really significant amount of federal funds, otherwise the new costs of compliance would be so great for the states that they would not sign the plan. Even with considerable federal aid, the states and local schools still bear the greatest burden of expense.

The formula proposed in the act promised to grow over five years to a maximum federal share of 40% of the average per-pupil expenditure for children in each state. Such maximums are rarely, if ever, met. Although the federal share has grown to approximately $12 billion in recent years, it still represents a minority share of all local, state and federal special education funding. However, in absolute terms, that amount of money buys a great deal of special education services, enough to be of critical value to the states. That is what we counted on in our plans.

In the original "Education of the Handicapped Act," a simple formula determined a certain sum that would be "authorized to be appropriated" each year up to $200 million. The money would be distributed in direct proportion to a state's population of school-aged children. It did not matter if it was serving many children with disabilities or only a few—total population of children was the guide.

The new bills, however—S. 6 for the Williams Senate Bill and H.R. 70 for the Brademas House Bill (an earlier version was H.R. 69)—each had a formula that tied a state's grant to the number of children they were serving in special education programs. States doing a more complete job would, therefore, receive more funding. Although negotiations over the formula and its distribution did not make the headlines in the professional literature, they were key to the act's approval. In legislative politics, the game is sometimes about carrots and sticks, and always about money.

The carrot of tying funding to the number of children actually enrolled in Special Education, as proposed in S. 6 and H.R. 70, was that a state that increased the number of children served, or served more children proportionately than other states, would receive more money. In addition, knowing how many children it was serving, a state or district could calculate ahead of time how much money it would receive if Congress appropriated a full federal share per child, and that gave them a specific target to urge upon their federal legislators. For example, if the federal share was $100 per child and the local district enrolled 1,000 children it would receive $100,000. If Congress appropriated only $50 per child, the amount would be halved, so the local education officials and parents knew exactly what the impact of the federal share would be on their programs. In the original Title VI (EHA), the money went to the state and the state could divide it as it chose, or spend it all from the state agency. In many states certain areas received more funding than others depending on politics, e.g. suburbs versus cities or rural areas.

Money Details

Since there was no information on the amount directly spent on children with disabilities—neither the states nor the federal government kept such figures—the basis of the formula determining the federal share per handicapped child was written into the bills as equal to the "Average Per-Pupil Expenditure" (APPE) for "regular" education in that state. (APPE multiplied by the number of children.) Each state's APPE was computed each year by statisticians in the federal Office of Education, by using data regarding state figures for salaries, instructional materials, transportation, etc. It generally did not include the cost of new construction, but it did factor in operating costs. Actually, the figure had ambiguities because the states did not all follow the same accounting patterns and the federal government had no mechanism for imposing order or auditing, other than for the use of federal funds.

We at BEH had sponsored an independent study of costs and reviewed other reports aimed at understanding more about the costs of special education. As a result, we estimated that special education costs, on average, about twice the amount spent on a non-disabled child. Some students, who required speech therapy only, for example, cost less than twice the amount, while the more severely handicapped cost more. Overall, twice the cost was a reasonable estimate based on the best available studies.

The formula in both the House and Senate bills provided that in the first year each child served in a state would receive a share equal to 5% of the national APPE. In the second year the share would grow to 10%, in the third year to 20%, in the fourth year to 30%, and in the fifth year, to 40%, where it would remain for subsequent years. In light of the estimate that special education was twice as expensive as regular education, these percentages of the costs for "regular" education, represented about half their value against special education costs, where the average cost was twice as expensive. For example the federal share might be 5% of the regular APPE, let's say $1,000. But the average special education cost would be twice that, $2,000, so the federal share of special ed would be only half of the real costs to the schools. That is why, even with the large growth of funding in recent years, the federal share is still relatively small in percentage terms.

It is interesting to note that in 2001, the Senate, led by Senator Jim Jeffords (Republican, VT), Senator Tom Harkin (Democrat, IA) and Senator Edward Kennedy (Democrat, MA), passed an amendment to the budget resolution over the objections of the Bush Administration, to try to reach the 40% figure. At the time, the $7 billion annual funding represented only about 15 percent of overall APPE. Senator Jeffords, an advocate of the special education legislation for 25 years, left the Republican Party. He became an Independent and voted with Democrats on organization issues regarding the Senate, allowing them to gain control of the chamber from Republicans.

While Jeffords disagreed with the President and his party on a number of issues, he identified the funding for children with disabilities as a major motivator, since he felt he had received positive indications of support. In the years since, big increases in the President's budget and tremendous interest in Congress in helping the states meet the demand for special education services have led to substantial growth in funds. By 2012, the appropriations approached $12.6 billion for grants to states for school-aged and preschool-aged children in the two major programs—an astonishing sum considering such humble origins.

When the program was first being considered by Congress, Wilbur Cohen, former Undersecretary and Secretary of HEW, asked me how much money I thought would be needed to have the impact I was hoping for, I summoned up my courage and told him the then astronomical sum of $1 billion, and he just nodded. As I mentioned earlier, Senator Everett Dirksen (Republican, IL) once said, "A billion here, a billion there, the first thing you know you are talking about real money." (Dirksen was kidding, but you could never tell with him.)

While the issue of a funding formula may seem obscure to most people interested in educating children, it is a key to virtually all Congressional spending. In education legislation, proposed formulas often pit the larger, urban states against rural or less wealthy states. Resolving the funding formula was therefore necessary before S. 6 and H.R. 70 could be passed by Congress.

Local versus State

The original versions of the bills used the formula described above as the basis for a single grant to each state, which would then be distributed by the respective State Education Agency. While Congress studied the legislation, school district administrators and local boards of education started to lobby for that money to be disseminated at the local level and not left to state agencies where politics could play a part in its disbursement.

There were internal political battles in many states between various areas and counties, often reflected in the party that might represent them. For example, in New York, there were always funding battles among the more rural "upstate" areas, the suburbs and New York City. In most states, the large urban centers never received a proportional share because the distribution of legislators favored the suburban and rural areas. As population across the nation grew and shifted to the suburbs, both rural and urban legislators found themselves fighting for a fair share against the wealthier communities and their political power.

Direct disbursement of funds to local school districts would result in more equitable distribution.

Gus Steinhilber, then Executive Director of the National School Boards Association, did a very good job of lobbying this issue for the school boards, and the House, generally more sympathetic to local concerns than the Senate, changed the proposed formula accordingly. Gus had worked in the Office of Education's Legislative group and was highly informed. [9]

The decision concerning distribution of funds transferred a good deal of political power to the local districts, which could, as mentioned above, calculate how many children were served, and push Congress for a federal share with full knowledge of how much they would receive.

Another important political variable in the distribution formula had to do with the calculation of the average per-pupil expenditure. Wealthier states generally spend more on education and would get more federal funds if state figures were used. If national numbers were used, the states which spent less on education would get more since they fell below the national average.

Because of the many features of this complex bill, the deliberations took several years, from 1972 to 1975. Toward the end of the process, I received a call from Jack Reed, Counsel to the House Committee on Education and Labor. He and I had been professional friends since Carl Perkins (Democrat, KY) had become chairman in 1967 and I had almost become a committee staff member. Reed wanted to discuss the formula and, not surprisingly, he was concerned about the potential impact on Kentucky.

9 Gus Steinhilber and Richard Smith on the Senate Education Staff, and Jack Duncan, who worked in the Rehab Agency, are not uncommon examples of how interchange of professionals takes place between the Executive and Legislative branches, increasing the sophistication of both. This process also happened on the House of Representatives' HEW appropriations subcommittee staff, where Fred Pflueger had earlier served in the HEW Finance Office. Readers may recall similar interchanges in Defense, Intelligence, and probably in every agency-related committee.

We in BEH had developed several theoretical distribution tables based on different assumptions and found that allowing a state to receive its share based either on the national average per-pupil expenditure or the state expenditure, whichever was higher, would work well for Kentucky and other "poorer" states. Of course, it took away some of the "pot" from the wealthier states, but they would still receive more than with a flat "national average" formula.

Reed also wanted at least some of the funding to go directly to the local school districts or, in Washington-speak, local education agencies (LEAs). The Senate seemed locked in on distribution to state agencies, so it was time to plant the seeds of compromise. Reed did not feel all of the funds had to go to local districts. One possibility discussed was that 50% of the sum a state received would pass through to LEAs another suggested 75%.

In the weeks that followed, discussions were held at many levels, with the Washington representatives of the Chief State School Officers (CSSO) —the heads of the education agency in each state; with the representatives of local education administrators and of state and local school boards; with unions, professional groups and parents; and with members of Congress and the Executive Branch—to name a few.

In deconstructing the outcome, it is generally impossible to say who played the crucial role or who made the decision that led to the final adoption by Congress. Many people are involved, and many of them feel that their part was critical. You hear lots of phrases bandied about: "I spoke with Congressman X or with Senator Y" and he/she assured me that our view would prevail, etc." "I've been working with John Doe or Mary Roe, Congressional staff members, and…" "Our testimony before the Committee was persuasive…"

My own belief is that Jack Reed, after meeting quietly with me and no other staff members present, including those of the relevant subcommittees, probably suggested the outcome to his "principal," Committee Chairman Carl Perkins, saying it would work reasonably well for Kentucky—

and that was that. Everyone else was singing the song, but the piano is generally played with only two hands.

The final version of the Act, after the "Conference Committee" ironed out any differences between the House and Senate bills, provided that for the fiscal year ending June 30, 1978, 50% of each states' allotment would be distributed by the states to LEAs, and for the fiscal year ending June 30, 1979 and each subsequent year, the figure would be 75%.

That result, I felt, was more powerful politically, giving virtually every member of the House of Representatives the opportunity to work directly toward funding for his or her local special education program in Washington and not in the state capital.

But that was only one aspect of what needed to be resolved before the act could become law.

Parents' and Children's Rights

Having established the fundamental premise of the Act, "Free, Appropriate, Public Education" and the political power available through a funding formula, Congress had to decide what should be included in a "federal" law, as opposed to a local or state statute. Since there is no federal Constitutional "Right to Education," the philosophical underpinning of the proposed Act was "equity"—equal protection under the law as provided by the Bill of Rights.

The ingredients of the bill were assembled based on the experiences of parents as they told their stories in Washington. Also involved were representatives from various organizations comprising the disability community, who carried on an educational campaign with a major assist from teachers and other professionals, particularly the Council for Exceptional Children. In addition, a number of important parts of the bill were based on the several court cases that had expanded children's educational rights.

The most fundamental right to be established was the equivalent of a "right to education"—a change in the public policy at state and local levels that had allowed children to be turned away from schools. While in some states, e.g., Maryland, courts found such a protection under the state constitution, the nationwide issue was decided in the parent's/children's favor in federal courts under a ruling that denial of educational opportunity violated the "equal protection" provisions of the Bill of Rights. As a result of these rulings, other states acceded to the act's terms to avoid expensive court cases that they would probably lose.

Being "excluded" was not the only situation held to violate the rights of children. Another occurred when they were placed in special education without prior parental notification and involvement. Sometimes this was done on the basis of testing, often severely biased against the test taker. Incredibly, there were instances in which children received intelligence tests in English although they did not speak English fluently. Other tests also were found to discriminate on the basis of disability, race and other factors. Even if parents were notified that their child was going to be placed in a special education program, they generally had no say about it, even if the placement seemed flawed. One powerful example I remember was the case of a child with cerebral palsy, who had normal or superior intelligence, being put in a class with children who were mentally retarded because "There is no other program."

The Individual Education Program

To redress this situation, the bill included provisions calling for parents to receive prior notification of testing and for the testing to be in the appropriate language. Most importantly, parents were to have a role in determining the education program which the bill required be developed for each child. This individual education program or plan became known as the IEP.

Although it has become the subject of some controversy because of the paperwork that has developed in some states and districts, the requirements of IEP in terms of the act that was ultimately passed were relatively simple.

A group of educators, including the child's teacher, a special education teacher and the school principal or a representative, such as a school psychologist, would work out a plan together. It would include overall goals, services to be offered, and provisions made for measuring the short-term objectives. This plan would then be discussed with the parents in a meeting, and while they did not have "veto" power, the intent of the legislation was for the school to respect and value their input.

The IEP provision also called for reviewing accomplishments on at least a yearly basis, and comprehensive testing every three years to determine the child's needs. Some school districts implemented these provisions effectively, using as little as a single sheet of paper; others elaborated them to byzantine proportions—we later found IEPs of 40 or more pages.

The IEP, agreed to by the parents, was the basis for determining that the education was, in fact, "appropriate" in accord with "Free, appropriate, public education." It is important to note that this determination was made at the local level, not by the federal or state governments, although any complaints about unnecessary paperwork were conveniently blamed on "the feds."

Impartial Hearings

Recognizing that disputes would occur concerning the services to be offered and their appropriateness, a major provision of the law created the process of "impartial hearings." If the parents or the school district wished, they could schedule a review by an "impartial" hearing officer. This officer would review the situation and make a decision that would be binding, although it still could be appealed by either party to a state level hearing officer. Finally, the parties could take their differences to Federal District Court, and ultimately through the Appeal Courts to the Supreme Court. A few cases have gone that route and made it all the way to the Supreme Court.

Some people have criticized the fact that local and state education agencies are allowed to form the lists of hearing officers, thereby "tilting" the process toward them; but in general, parents have not challenged the hearing officers' impartiality.

This particular portion of the act is another example that legislation often involves compromise and practical limitations, and that even the most effective and useful law cannot be perfect. School districts have been more concerned by this process than parents, fearing not only the cost of services they might be ordered to provide, but also the potential costs of litigation, which included the expenses incurred by the parents, if they won the case.

The latter provision was included in the law because, in general, school districts are more capable of paying legal costs than individual parents and so this provision helped balance out a financial deterrent to appealing. (A provision further clarifying parents' rights to recover costs when they prevailed in hearings or court cases was later added by Senator Lowell Weicker (Republican, CT) when he chaired the Senate Subcommittee on Disability Policy. (that subcommittee was the re-titled heir to the original William's/Randolph, subcommittee.)

Weicker's chairmanship of the committee was very significant because he was a strong advocate. He and his wife had a child with a disability. He stood strongly against the Reagan Administration's attempts to change the regulations, weakening the protections for parents and children. He also would have opposed amendments to the law that had the same effect, so while they were rumored, they were not forthcoming. Senator Robert Stafford (Republican, VT) was then the full committee chairman, and these New England "progressive Republicans" did not march to Reagan's drum. Weicker, like Representative Jim Jeffords, became an Independent.

This establishment of an appeal process and naming of hearing officers received much scrutiny as the bill was being developed. School authorities naturally objected to it, since they were used to making unilateral decisions. One staff attorney on the Senate Committee on Labor and Public Welfare, Nik Edes, was especially concerned about parent rights. He felt there should be a special "entity," as he called it, which would hold these hearings wherever they occurred within a state, rather than allowing local districts to create a list of hearing officers. In Edes' view, the "entity" would be more objective.

As an attorney, Edes, like a good many of his fellow professionals, became deeply interested in the issue of equal treatment under the law for children with disabilities. While they played a positive role in the development of the legislation, their practical background in special education and education administration was often limited.

While I respected Edes' intent, I knew it simply was not practical. As an example, in my native state, New York, an Edes "entity" might have to hold a hearing on Long Island one day and then have to travel more than 400 miles to Buffalo for the next. With millions of children receiving special education and even a small number of hearings, the entity or even several entities would be on the road constantly, and the job probably wouldn't appeal to many qualified professionals. Deemed infeasible, the proposal was dropped as the bill moved forward.

Child Find and Education with Non-Disabled Children

With its emphasis on "rights," the Education for All Handicapped Children Act was unprecedented in education law. It combined the growing support for civil rights with federal funding, while trying to find a middle ground between federal procedural standards and local decision making in education.

One of the expansions of children's rights was the provisions for "child find." The states, in agreeing to participate under the act's terms, had an affirmative responsibility to establish systems to find and identify children with disabilities. This included children who were not yet in school as well as those enrolled who were not receiving appropriate educational services. The "child find" provisions resulted in local and state schools beginning screening and other programs for children about to enter schools.[10]

Least Restrictive Alternative

An important provision of the Act, combining its emphasis on improved educational opportunity and its civil rights protections, called for children with disabilities to be educated, where appropriate, with non-disabled children. Separating people with disabilities from society at large has a long history, including the development of special hospitals and institutions in the 19th and 20th centuries, following even more extreme societal exclusions such as expulsion from the family, being locked in basements, etc.

In the period preceding PL 94-142, most children receiving special education did so in separate classrooms or separate schools. Children with moderate to severe mental retardation or emotional/behavioral disabilities often were placed in separate state schools or institutions. Many of these places were poorly maintained and operated, and exposés of their miserable conditions led to court actions and the return of children to their home communities, supported by public opinion, but generally still in special facilities.

Children who were deaf or blind also found education placements most often available in state schools. In general, those programs were superior to those offered in the state schools and institutions for the children mentioned above; however, they were often far from home, requiring young children to be separated from their families.

With this background in mind, I spoke often in favor of the approach, eventually adopted in PL 94-142, that would offer a continuum of placement options and educational opportunities, preferably in the local school district. The idea was based on an article published by Professor Evelyn Deno of the University of Minnesota, which described the "continuum" approach and its possible characteristics—in terms of the final bill, the most "appropriate" situation.

10 Note: provisions for preschool programming are discussed elsewhere, not under this section on rights.

For some children a special hospital or school might be "appropriate." For others it might be a special class or perhaps part-time placement in a special class or resource room with other periods spent in a regular classroom. Still other children might be "appropriately" educated in regular classrooms, perhaps with some additional specialized attention.

The key to deciding which settings were most appropriate resided in the IEP process, with local educators in consultation with parents coming up with the best possible program.. Periodic reviews were built into the IEP process as written in the law. To make certain that children were not arbitrarily separated, the act called on schools to educate children with disabilities alongside children who were not disabled, wherever "appropriate."

The phrase, "least restrictive environment," grew out of the court decisions in the early 70s while the bills leading to PL 94-142 were being developed by Congress. In cases such as PARC, mentioned earlier, the consent decree called for an end to Pennsylvania's practice of separating all children with mental retardation from public school settings. Recognizing that children differed in degree of disability, the court language called for the least restrictive setting to be offered—that is, a setting which could provide the required services, but be as close to home and still assure that the education provided was "appropriate."

The concept—that a determination has to be made for each individual child with disability—has become the basis for much controversy and, some would claim, fundamental changes in the special education. Some see these changes as positive, others negative, still others are uncertain as to the effects. (See Part IV for my discussion of "appropriate" with members of Congress.)

Provisions for Younger and Older Children

When we began planning and drafting S. 6 and HR. 70 I hoped we could include children of preschool age under the requirements for free, appropriate, public education. There also was a group of children older than the traditional range of public school requirements, ages five to 17 who, because of their special needs, would require additional education, perhaps to age 21.

The provision was challenged by members of Congress, including some sympathetic with the legislation. The reason was that while children between the ages of 5 to 17 were covered under state laws, many states did not offer education to children aged 3 to 5 or younger; nor did they guarantee education to those who were between 18 and 21 years old. Since the philosophic and constitutional underpinnings of the bills were that children were being denied equal treatment under the law, that argument would not hold for situations where children without disabilities were not granted access to public education either. In recognition of the value of such programming, however, the act signed into law allowed the states to spend the funds on children aged 3 to 5 and 18 to 21, although they could not count them in the formula for gaining federal funds.

In later actions Congress developed special programs of grants for preschool and even younger children, ages 0 to 2, to encourage such programming. Similarly, many states extended their services to children older than 17, and provisions requiring the development of transition programs to work and post-secondary training came into being accordingly.

Summary

The final version of the bills that became PL 94-142 blended many concepts—financial, administrative, educational and civil rights. The views of parents and children's rights were paramount, e.g. the IEP and requirements for "related services." Teachers' concerns that they would be involved in developing the educational plan with decisions at the local level were an assurance of "local control." The requirement for "no exclusion," which became the fundamental FAPE and had to be guaranteed by the states in order to participate in the grant program, met the federal court-established requirements in "PARC" and "Mills."

Both positive and negative observers pronounced the bill as "landmark" legislation, which would establish educational civil rights and at the same time create a major new federal investment in special education. Major change in Washington always attracts supporters and naysayers. Many powerful individuals and groups are threatened by it—financially, ideologically, etc. As a result, passage of the bills in the House and Senate and ultimate signing them into law were not foregone conclusions. It took a great deal of time and effort, requiring beating the drum to rally public support and working diligently behind the scenes in the corridors of power that ultimately came to a head during a time of great political upheaval—the resignation of President Nixon and the run up to the 1976 presidential election.

PART FOUR

Congressional Action and Implementation

To pass the bill that would become PL 94-142, it was necessary to develop a consensus in Congress that the legislation was needed, wanted and feasible. Support was very strong among parents and special educators, but school administrators, school board members and some elected officials at the local and state levels were wary. More significantly, from the start, the Nixon Administration opposed a new education grant program to the states. The basic argument was that education was a state responsibility. An added factor to the resistance was that the bill raised the specter of "federal control," an ongoing debate between Democrats and Republicans regarding the role of government that continues to this day.

At the time, the feeling among the political cognoscenti was that an important underlying factor for the resistance was that many members of Nixon's team felt that education, especially for the disadvantaged, was "a Johnson thing," and not something they advocated or would ever get credit for. They had already been convinced by the Office of Education and higher education forces to continue and even expand the existing higher education grant and loan programs, something which many conservatives thought was akin to a loss of sanity.

H.R. 70, the Brademas bill and S. 6, the Williams bill, were actually considered over the period of two Congressional sessions, being reintroduced in 1974, when the 94th Congress convened. (H.R. 70 had been H.R. 69 in the earlier Congress.) During these years there were periodic hearings and all the major interest groups had their chance to speak. As mentioned in the previous section, the local school boards made the case for funds being distributed to local agencies rather than to the states in the House. Concerns about the IEP process were raised in both chambers of Congress.

Gradually, most major education groups came to back the legislation, albeit reluctantly in some cases. I worked hard with a variety of organizations to encourage their support. The American Federation of Teachers, for example, had concerns at the grassroots level about adding children with disabilities to the classroom teachers' burdens; and I met with then president Albert Shanker and his aide, later president, Sandra Feldman, to work on the problems.

The Chief State School Officers (CSSO), the superintendents of education for each state, clearly did not want the responsibility and costs for having to educate children with disabilities, although they could not admit that openly. They feared—and with good reason—that the federal government would not provide enough funds to do the job. Ironically, most were already expected or required to do that job, but they had always been able to avoid the responsibility either through loopholes in state laws, or simply by ignoring the laws with impunity.

When I spoke at the national meeting of the Chief State School Officers, I challenged them to become the leaders who brought children with disabilities fully into the education system, an accomplishment for which they could rightly be proud. I urged them to join in support for the goal of educating all "handicapped" children by 1980.

There were a few voices raised in support. One was Gregory Anrig from Massachusetts[11] and another, Arthur Mallory of Missouri. But Jack Nix, then the CSSO of Georgia and a long-time advocate for Vocational Education, resented that we had "earmarked" 10% of the federal government's funding from voc-ed programs for students with disabilities, and his tone and approach were negative.

As a result, the CSSO organization did not pass a resolution supporting Education for All Handicapped Children by 1980, and only reluctantly did not oppose the legislation. Later it fired its in-house lobbyist because of concerns that he had led the CSSO into being too positive about the bill. Perhaps the final straw was the decision of Congress to provide most of the money to the local districts rather than through CSSO offices, but it undoubtedly also included other requirements in the bill, such as parental notification, IEP teams, and impartial hearings.

The organizations of state legislatures and Governors were also not anxious to have to come up with new sources of revenue, and mostly feared the proposed legislation, although there were some very strong advocates as well, particularly in some of the state legislatures.

---

11 Greg Anrig had been the head of the Office of Civil Rights in the Office of Education in the mid 1960s and when asked by Senator Strom Thurmond (Republican, SC) how his state was supposed to comply with a desegregation order affecting a segregated school on a coastal island, famously replied, "Would you believe a yellow boat with red blinking lights?"

After Nixon's resignation because of Watergate, the Republicans in Washington under President Gerald Ford were still opposing the bills. There were some key Republican legislators, however, who were strong advocates for the legislation, including Albert Quie, the ranking member of the minority on the House Education Committee, and Senator Robert Stafford, ranking minority member on the Senate Committee (later chairman, when Republicans became the majority party), as was Senator Jacob Javits.

Developing a consensus was one thing, implementing the act and getting the states to agree to its requirements would be something else altogether.

CHAPTER 13

The Final Stages

Bringing about a consensus of support for the pending bills involved the work of many people. Lisa Walker, Jack Duncan, and lead staff in the Senate and House worked tirelessly on behalf of the legislation introduced by their "principals." They met with any group that might play a significant role in drumming up support—administrators, teachers, parents, and more, not to mention the staff of other legislators that had ideas, questions or concerns.

Judy Heumann, founder of Disabled in Action, a New York City group, joined the Senate staff in 1974 and provided additional backing for the legislation, as well as encouraging the active participation of people with disabilities. Heumann was later nominated and confirmed as Assistant Secretary of Education for Special Education and Rehabilitative Services in 1993.

Fred Weintraub and Alan Abeson from CEC gave a great deal of technical assistance to "the Hill" staff members and also took part in discussions which included the Washington representatives of any of the organizations the legislation would impact. Paul Marchand, Executive Director of The Arc, (formerly the National Association for Retarded Citizens), headed a coalition of groups supporting the legislation. Together they established a grassroots network of teachers and advocates involved in contacting local legislators and others with influence. Weintraub and Abeson also worked at the state level with the model statute they developed, which increased the demand for federal aid.

The group of education and special education organizations who were "stakeholders," to use a modern cliché, included parent groups and disability organizations. Of great importance, too, were the newly emerging groups of persons with disabilities wanting to speak for themselves.

Dr. Frank Bowe, first head of the American Coalition of Citizens with Disabilities, (he identified himself as a deaf man,) an organization that attempted to bring together persons with disabilities as a political force, also worked hard to develop "consumer" support. The effort to secure passage of the bill helped Bowe and his organization become stronger and more visible, and led to them playing a greater role in advising some succeeding Administrations on policy.

The broader coalition of groups interested in disability policy that Marchand and Bowe led included representatives of state-based organizations, the associations of Governors, state legislators, school boards, etc. They met regularly to debate issues like the IEP, impartial hearings, formulas and other provisions of the law that presented new tasks and responsibilities.

I met regularly with them and all of us at BEH, often with the involvement of Bob Herman and Harvey Liebergott, who ran our program supporting parent information centers, provided updates and gave insights into the process and answered questions from all quarters.

During the five years leading up to 1975, I made hundreds of speeches to relevant groups urging support of the goal of education for all handicapped children by 1980 and support for S. 6 and H.R. 70 as a major step toward meeting that goal.

In addition, we at BEH also made it a priority to support organizations involved in activities designed to provide information about the need for the proposed legislation and its characteristics. Grants for such "training" purposes went to groups as diverse as the National Association of State Directors of Special Education (NASDE), the Education Commission of the States, the American Federation of Teachers, and the association of State Boards of Education. We assumed these grants and activities would build favorable attitudes toward the bills and we were proven correct for the most part.

Harvey Liebergott

I have mentioned Harvey Liebergott before as someone whose gift for reaching out to parents of children with disabilities was a tremendous asset to BEH. Besides his own experience teaching deaf students at Gallaudet University, he also had insight into speech, language and hearing disorders, through his wife Jackie, who had a Ph.D. in that area (she retired last year as president of Emerson College in Boston).

Liebergott played a unique role as our "ambassador" to parents of children with disabilities. They learned that he cared and that they could trust him, and so that helped their vision of the Bureau as an ally. All too often, parents had learned to be wary of school administrators at local and state levels, seeing them as resistant to their goals, (and their children). The parents were an effective lobby for the legislation, as they had been for virtually every piece of local, state and federal programming. Working with Martha Ziegler, who had a daughter with autism and had formed a parents' coalition advocating for children with all disabilities in Massachusetts, Liebergott also effectively used small grants from our information program to encourage similar parent coalitions in other states.

Internships and Stacking the Deck in BEH's Favor

For some time, BEH had supported programs that provided internships in Washington for special educators interested in policy. One of these was through the Institute for Educational Leadership (IEL), associated with the George Washington University, but operated independently by its director, Samuel Halperin, formerly the Deputy Assistant Secretary for Legislation for HEW. (He has already appeared in these pages during the discussion of the fight over creating BEH.)

Halperin's goal was to improve and expand public policy for programs of education, particularly education for the economically disadvantaged, and he had firsthand expertise and good rapport with Congressional staff and many members from his HEW days. When he left the government, he established the Educational Staff Seminar as one part of IEL. It took "Hill" staffers to visit sites funded by federal dollars that they had helped create. There they had the opportunity to speak with people actually involved at the grassroots level. If a trip involved special education, I would often be invited. Similarly, other program heads were invited on trips to the sites reflecting their own interests. These visits served a double purpose—providing a fuller education and also building linkages between "Hill" and Executive branch players.

IEL also organized seminars and discussions of programs and policy, which worked well and, in contrast to much that is going on in Washington today, fostered civility and friendship in inter-party discussions.

In addition, IEL recruited bright, articulate male and female graduate students and young professionals for "fellowships," placing them in Washington policy-making organizations and associations which composed the education lobby in Washington. As a result, we had several special education specialists in agencies like the National Association of State School Boards, and they played a significant role in helping communicate the message of a need for improved and expanded education for children with disabilities.

Some of the institutions of higher education we funded also had Washington intern programs. An early leader was Syracuse University under Professor Dan Sage. Some of his fellows came into the Bureau itself, as well as some other Washington-based organizations. Later, Professor Phil Burke, a BEH alumnus, began a policy program at the University of Maryland that placed bright graduate students in "Hill" staff positions where they had significant impact on federal policy, which continued in the years after PL 94-142 was passed. Dr. Jane West, for example, became a permanent staff member on the Disability Policy Subcommittee chaired by Senator Weicker and played an important role in improving and expanding, and occasionally saving, federal programs for children and adults with disabilities.

Commissioner of Education, Terrell "Ted" Bell

As the process moved toward its conclusive votes in both chambers of Congress, the House of Representatives held hearings and asked the members of the Administration to testify. Commissioner of Education Terrell "Ted" Bell (later Secretary of Education in the Reagan Administration), was to be the lead witness, and I was to accompany him.

Bell and I had met as colleagues early in the Nixon Administration when we were, of necessity, rivals fighting for parts of the Office of Education budget, but we always had friendly relations based on mutual respect. As head of the bureau for elementary and secondary programs, he had a much larger domain than I, especially the billion-dollar-plus Title I of ESEA.

As a former school superintendent in a prosperous Salt Lake City suburb, Bell had a sense of the needs of children with disabilities and was generally inclined to be helpful. On the other hand, he was essentially a conservative. Perhaps the label "compassionate conservative" would fit him best; his bottom line was conservative nonetheless.

I think there was a considerable gap between his friendly, easygoing persona—he liked to portray himself as a simple country boy—and his inner drive to succeed. Bell was of short stature, and he would kid around about it. I recall him at one speaking engagement bringing the microphone down to his mouth level and saying, "Let's adjust this for normal-sized people." He had also served in the Marine Corps, so the easygoing Mormon exterior masked a tough core.

Bell came to the Office of Education during the Nixon years as Associate Commissioner for Elementary and Secondary Education (BESE) after serving as the State Superintendent of Education of Utah, following his tenure as a local superintendent. At the time, the Bureau directors were each Associate Commissioners and part of the career bureaucracy.

Later, in the terms of Nixon and Ford, they became politically appointed Deputy Commissioners.

When Bell and I began our terms as Associate Commissioners, we held the same rank. The Commissioner who appointed us, James Allen, had served as the State Commissioner in New York. Allen was in hot water with the Nixon White House from the beginning. Southern conservatives, a key component in the Republican's "Southern Strategy," found he had supported busing children in New York to break the patterns of school segregation, and considered him a "fox in the chicken coop." When the first budget he submitted was sharply reduced by the White House and its fiscal arm, the Bureau of the Budget, Allen felt betrayed. He thought he had been promised much more when he was recruited.

Allen also refused to keep his own feelings about the war in Vietnam to himself. While on a speaking visit to a university campus, he criticized the "incursion into Cambodia" as unjustified and was promptly fired. Ted Bell was named Acting Commissioner and then Commissioner. He had had a rapid rise, from his ingenuous beginnings as a simple country boy to the top education job in government.

As a former local superintendent, Bell was generally sympathetic to the need for programming for children with disabilities; although, as head of BESE, he had had his own programs, primarily aimed at children who were "disadvantaged," and they were his real concern. Although he described himself as less than 100% involved, he and his family followed the Mormon church traditions—led by Mrs. Bell—of concern for private social welfare and assisting others.

In any case, Commissioner Bell convinced the education community, including Senator Stafford, with whom I discussed this, that he was a reasoned advocate for education in hostile Administrations—Nixon's and later Reagan's, where he was named Secretary of Education in a department the President planned to abolish. At the same time he demonstrated the loyalty necessary to win and maintain important appointments from his Republican masters, so he successfully managed to have it both ways—

a rare feat and a credit to his survival instincts. I must confess, though, that as I saw Bell perform his "I am a good guy trapped by a less savory administrative policy" act in two Republican Administrations, I became a bit cynical. [12]

For me, serving in Republican and Democratic Administrations was a less challenging task because I was not a presidential appointee. I had been hired as a professional and occupied top positions as a career executive. That allowed me to maintain a certain independence and to make decisions based on conscience, without fear of being fired. While I could be transferred into a position akin to a transfer to Antarctica, there would have been some political and constituent uproar, (as later events would demonstrate.) Such a "demotion" might also be subject to civil service scrutiny if it were protested and, if found to be a blatant political move unjustified by performance, prove embarrassing to the Administration.

Bell knew that I had been committed to comprehensive federal legislation assuring education for every disabled child since we met at the beginning of the Nixon Administration. He also knew that I was working behind the scenes with Congress and in the field to shape the legislation that the White House opposed, but as long as I did it quietly and professionally, he did not try to rein me in. Others in the Administration, however, bore me ill will, even if they did not find it possible to remove me, primarily because there was bipartisan support for my efforts in Congress as well as overwhelming support from parents and professionals. They would take their best shot as things unraveled in the final days of the Nixon presidency.

Hearings Before the House Select Education Subcommittee

When the Select Education Subcommittee, chaired by John Brademas with Al Quie as the "Ranking Minority Member," began its final set of hear-

12 For a fuller discussion see my review of Bell's book, "The Thirteenth Man: A Reagan Cabinet Memoir," in the Teachers College Record," vol. 91, no.2, Winter, 1989.

ings on the legislation, Commissioner Bell read his statement (the official Office of Management and Budget line). He suggested that while the legislation was well-intentioned, it would lead to over-involvement of the federal government in the education system, it would be much more costly than recognized, and it suffered from other flaws. I don't think he really opposed the legislation personally, but it was a mark of his political skill that some people felt he supported it and others thought he opposed it.

The committee members listened politely to his statement on behalf of the Administration. Then Quie and Brademas asked the Commissioner if he would mind if they posed a few questions to me. Bell agreed and the real dialogue on provisions of the act began. For more than an hour Bell sat quietly by. He did not get up and leave and take me with him, as he might have—however much it might have irritated the committee—and let me have my say; and I am grateful to him for that.

Part of the hearing process, often not recognized by the public at large, is the building of "legislative history," which can come into play in court decisions establishing what Congress intended in legislation. It was in that context that Quie asked me about the Individual Education Plans the bill proposed. Many school officials had fears that the IEP would be a kind of contract guaranteeing positive results, and that parents would sue the schools if their children did not succeed. Quie wanted to know whether that was the agency's view, since we would be enforcing the law and drafting the specific "regulations" that would elaborate on the act's provisions. Federal regulations, once "promulgated," have the force of law.

I answered that we had examined it with our counsel and felt it was not a contract for improvement; it was, arguably, a contract to deliver the services agreed upon. The bill's provisions called for a team of school personnel to evaluate a child's special education needs, prescribe a program of services, and then follow up on progress on at least an annual basis. The parents, who would be part of that discussion, did not have veto power, but they could appeal an unfavorable decision by the IEP team to an "impartial hearing officer." School officials had warned Congress that parents would see the IEP as guaranteeing improvement, not just providing services, and Quie was satisfied, having made that point clear in the hearing record.

The questioning moved on, touching on the formula for distribution on a state or local level of the moneys appropriated. I supported a distribution to both, with the state using funds in ways that the direct granting of small sums to small school districts might not allow, such as regional programs for low-incidence disabilities, regional resource centers and instructional material centers, training activities for teachers from various school districts, and similar items where state funding seemed to make sense. I did not push for a given percentage, since it was clear that the House and Senate were going to thrash out their differences, although I supported direct grants to local school districts as part of the formula.

Then Quie asked me about a key phrase which appeared in the bill, where children were to be provided a "free, appropriate, public education." There had been concerns raised that "federal bureaucrats" would decide what was appropriate for every school district, imposing greatly on local control of the schools, guaranteed by the absence of language regarding it in the Constitution.

I replied by telling him a story about Bill Klem, the great Major League Baseball umpire, who had recently retired. Klem was always referred as "The Dean of Major League Umpires." After his retirement Klem was interviewed and asked to name his biggest mistake while officiating. He replied that he had made none. The incredulous reporter said, "But Mr. Klem, you must have called tens of thousands of pitches as balls and strikes—surely you must have missed one." Klem replied, "Until I called it—it was nothing."

Quie knew me well enough—and I was grinning, I am sure, as I told the story—so he understood I was kidding and replied in kind, "That is exactly what I was afraid of."

The real answer, as the reader knows by now, is that the locally developed IEP was the basis of what was "appropriate." If the school chose it and the parent agreed, that created an operational definition of what was "appropriate." There was no federal involvement or role in the process.

That, to me, is one of the beauties of the law as it emerged: It provided a strong federal impetus for improved and expanded educational opportunity, but it did not interfere with the child-based decisions at the local level—except of course, by setting the expectation that services would be provided and prohibiting obviously discriminatory actions. Even those actions, for example, testing Latino children in English, would trigger a full review by the Office of Civil Rights, and possibly a court review, rather than just a solitary decision by a BEH specialist.

We also discussed the provision for "related services," which I had worked to have included in the draft bills. These included such things as physical and occupational therapy, psychological services and counseling, social work services, speech, language and hearing disorder treatment (not medical in nature), and such services necessary to make special education programming effective for a given child.

Fred Weintraub was less than enthusiastic about this provision, fearing that the backlash from school officials would hurt the larger bill—not an unreasonable position. Weintraub also felt classroom instruction was the most important feature of special education and considered related services an extraneous feature—valuable, but not essential.

I felt that to have a program for a child with orthopedic disabilities or mental health problems, for example, and not provide that child with the appropriate therapies as part of the overall plan was defeating the whole purpose. Congress eventually agreed and included the provision, but made clear that medical treatments, such as surgery, could not be paid for by the "education funds" appropriated under the act.

These provisions became an issue on several occasions after the act was passed. One came in relation to the provision of "counseling" and "psychological" services. Were psychiatrists, who have an M.D., ruled out because of the bar on "medical" services? In the regulations we allowed that such services were allowable, as well as counseling and psychological services.

The Supreme Court Weighs In

Later, after the act was implemented, a case reached the Supreme Court dealing with what is known as "clean, intermittent, catheterization." This is the process of helping a child (or adult) release urine using a catheter when the individual's physical condition does not allow for independent control of this function. Some children had been barred from school—denied an education—because the school did not want to provide this service through a school nurse or other personnel.

We proposed in the regulations that it should be provided under related services and that it was not a medical procedure. After all, older children and adults could self-catheterize, and parents and aides often provided the service routinely at home and elsewhere.

This provision got very careful attention from the nation's first Secretary of Education, Shirley Hufstedler and her special assistant Judy Wagner. Secretary Hufstedler, who joined the Carter Administration after serving on the U.S. Court of Appeals in California, hired a number of excellent attorneys to help staff her office and to be of counsel. Wagner was one these legal eagles and she was polite, courteous, intelligent, reasoned and fastidious when it came to the law and to the Secretary's responsibilities under the law. She earned my respect quickly.

After careful review and a meeting between the Secretary and me to discuss the issue, that provision was included in the regulations. Wagner and the Secretary were right to pay careful attention to the issue because, sure enough, it became the focus of court battles all the way to the Supreme Court, which upheld the regulations. Needless to say, there were considerable smiles in our camp when that decision came down.

President Ford Faces the Decision

Despite positive hearings and strong outside support from parents and education groups, the bills seemed to bog down in their respective houses of Congress, although John Brademas told me that he felt certain they would pass eventually. I am not sure anyone knows exactly why there might have been a slowdown. Certainly, the near impeachment and ultimate resignation of President Nixon put many items on hold while the dust settled.

Once it did, the White House under President Ford was looking toward the upcoming election. Ford had a tenuous position as a candidate. Many people felt his pardon of Nixon was a political favor to the former President; some observers even speculated that it was agreed upon as a condition to Ford's being named Vice President. Others accepted Ford at his word that he saw it necessary to promote "healing" and to move on.

Ford had had a long career in the House, rising to Republican Leader, but he was not seen as a brilliant or charismatic commander, rather more like a solid workhorse—steady and loyal to his party before all else. The later satires by comedian Chevy Chase, among others, which painted him as dumb and clumsy, were not really fair. Ford was a graduate of Yale Law School and a skier well into his 60s. But like President George W. Bush, he did not project a public image of someone interested in intellectual pursuits, books or the world of ideas. Lyndon Johnson famously remarked of Ford that he could not "walk and chew gum at the same time." Sources close to Johnson tell me he used a different verb than "walk," but one not suitable for a "PG-rated" book.

The Education for All Handicapped Children Act, as has been noted earlier, was a major step forward in federal education legislation. It represented a major financial commitment, a fundamental change for the schools which had historically limited or avoided special education programs, and most significantly, a much more aggressive federal role in setting standards for local schools, although, as noted, the final decisions on children's programs were still a local responsibility. These factors added up to some uneasiness in Congress because of the opposition of some Chief State School Officers, and by some state school board members and government officials. The issue of "unfunded mandates" was being articulated along with the many voices of support.

As advocates, the supporters of the legislation wanted to put President Ford and Republican members to the test—would they go beyond verbal warnings about the legislation and, in the President's case, veto the bill if passed? I believe Brademas was of a similar mind. He did not articulate all his views in his conversations with me, just his overall commitment to seeing it passed and his belief that the President would not veto it. While disability advocates might not tilt an election, vetoing bills for educating children with disabilities might look terrible in the press.

Thus, when the legislation moved to the floors of the House and Senate, it had very little opposition—a handful of votes against it, seven Republicans in the Senate and seven in the House, and so the ball was in President Ford's court.

"No Thank You"

A message came down from the Secretary of HEW's office through the Commissioner of Education, Ted Bell, directing the preparation of a veto message. I could not bring myself to do that task and called Bell and asked him to find someone else to do that—there were any number of people in the Planning and Budgeting offices who could spell out the Administration's objections to the bill. I offered to write a message expressing the president's views if he decided to sign the bill. Bell accepted my request—another sign of his respect for me and my views—which I appreciated.

I don't have any idea who eventually wrote the veto message. Knowing how these things go, there was probably a draft prepared in HEW, then modified or re-written in the Bureau of the Budget, and probably massaged again by White House staff's domestic policy and speech writers. In any event, the final product was brief—only a few paragraphs in length.

Still, President Ford signed the bill into law, but without any formal bill-signing ceremony—a disappointment even to seasoned professionals like me who look for their "moment in the sun" at a White House signing of a law they helped construct. The message he sent accompanying the signing was the veto message, spelling out the Administration's views that had been presented a number of times to Congress and the public. It ended with the words, "I am reluctantly signing...."

That night we had a small celebration at a local restaurant, and Lisa Walker, Jack Duncan, Fred Weintraub and some others raised a few toasts to Public Law 94-142. It was not a drunken, rowdy scene, but rather a tired yet happy gathering of friends quietly celebrating the end of what amounted to a three-year battle. We knew we had accomplished something important.

***

Some years later, I was boarding a flight to Denver when I noticed a cluster of Secret Service agents. (Not many people wore buttons in their ears before the iPod era.) As I looked more carefully, I recognized President Ford, seemingly quite frail, with a blanket over his shoulders, sitting in an unlighted window seat in the first row. He was heading toward his residence in the Vail, Colorado area.

When the plane was in the air and things were settled, I asked a Secret Service agent if the President would allow me a few words and explained my former government role. Ford graciously acceded and we spoke about former Representative and Governor of Minnesota, Al Quie, who I knew was a friend. He brightened and as we chatted I reminded him of PL 94-142, The Education for All Handicapped Children Act, and asked if he had any recollections about the possibility of a veto. He smiled, shook his head negatively, and said, "I had pretty much on my plate in those days."

CHAPTER 14

"From Rhetoric to Reality"

BEH was responsible for developing the federal regulations that "fleshed out" and filled in the gaps in the law. There is virtually no law that stands just as written, especially one with complex, operational features. Regulations ("regs") are written by the Executive Branch following the enactment of the law, which provide explanations about some of the meaning and intent and also add stipulations for compliance with the law's provisions. Once promulgated—reg-speak for "printed in the Federal Register" —Congress sometimes feels that the regulations distort the meaning of the Act, reflecting, for example, dissident views in the Executive Branch. The "regs" have the force of law, unless specifically contradicted by additional Congressional legislation.

During the 1970s, the Nixon Administration tried to ignore Congressional intent on a number of issues, even ones as fundamental as spending the funds that Congress appropriated. The Nixon team held up money for programs it did not support and argued it had the right to do so despite the separation of powers in the Constitution that ceded that responsibility to Congress. That issue went to Court, and President Nixon lost and had to release the funds.

The net result was that Congress began making legislation more and more specific, dotting "i's" and crossing "t's" in order to try to avoid regulations which changed its intent. The more specific the legislation became, the more difficult it was in some instances to administer in a real world of "grays" rather than "black and whites."

PL 94-142 had a good bit of legislative specificity, but it still left a great deal to be spelled out, and the task for the Bureau was a major one; especially so, since many administrators were concerned about the law's requirements and many parents wanted to make sure the schools complied with the law.

Developing the Regulations

We established a task force to consider our approach and assigned the major job of writing the "regs" to Tom Irvin, a conscientious, careful workman who had worked previously in the Minnesota state department of education and had much practical knowledge of how special education worked in state and local districts.

I wanted to involve as many people as possible in developing the "regs." First, I felt they would surely be improved by the input and second, I wanted "the field," as we called it, to feel ownership in the final product. It would not be something handed down from on high by faceless bureaucrats.

The first step was to gather groups of people to discuss the philosophy and principles behind various aspects of the law, such as child find, least restrictive environment, the IEP, the parental appeals process, etc. Each major concept was examined by a group and the results of everyone's views synthesized.

After the draft regulations were written, mostly by Irvin, we then had a second round of meetings, to discuss them specifically. Various constituencies reviewed these drafts, including parents, teachers, administrators, attorneys who had been involved, and Capitol Hill staff. In all, we estimated about 1,000 people participated.

It would not be too much of an exaggeration to say this took place over a few "dead bodies" of the Office of Education's legal staff and related central offices, because it was almost the exact opposite of the usual way of developing regulations. The ordinary routine was to do it internally and in secret. The rationale was that if the process were open to outsiders, special interests would inject their views. (I can't help smiling at the irony of how times had changed by the Bush II Administration. The process of policy development on energy that took place under Vice President Cheney was essentially accomplished by outside special interests—the energy companies (environmentalists not invited). The list of participants never was revealed to the public, despite futile attempts by the media through court challenges all the way to the Supreme Court).

Once the internal deliberations were complete, a draft of the regulations would be published and then a period allowed for comment. The executive branch would decide what comments, if any, to adopt, and then the final version would be promulgated.

We took a different route, making everything very visible to all and involving people with divergent views in the topic discussions and the draft reviews. This openness provided a counter to the possibility of undue influence.

The proof of the value of this process was that the regulations stood the scrutiny of the practical world and the judicial system; later, when the Reagan Administration tried to dismantle them, thousands of parents protested and successfully blocked the dismantling. They clearly still felt ownership in the law and these federal policies almost a decade later.

Implementation Concerning State Plans

For a state to receive federal funds it had to sign a plan whose format followed the provisions of the law as implemented by the regulations. These plans were very detailed and required that the state promise it would comply with the various stipulations for assuring "a free, appropriate, public education." For many states that meant changing policy and/or state law.

In a number of cases, the major sticking point was the IEP impartial hearing officer reviews. New York and Texas were two states balking about that issue, and I recall becoming personally involved in to trying to resolve it.

New York

The Commissioner of Education in New York has certain judicial powers in elementary and secondary schools and in higher education.

Several years ago, for example, the Commissioner and the state regents dismissed the Board of Trustees of Adelphi University, a private institution, in a situation that involved allegations of over-compensating the president and conflicts of interest by some board members. The ability of a state education officer to make such a decision involving a private school or university is highly unusual and, to my knowledge, virtually unique to New York.

Given that background, the Commissioner at the time, Gordon Ambach, felt that appeals arising from a special education hearing, if they reached the state level—beyond the local decision by a hearing officer—should be handled by his office. PL 94-142 called for an independent hearing officer at the state level, however, whose decision would be binding, although it could be appealed by either party to the federal district court. Ambach told me that New York law could not be countermanded.

I held that I could not approve New York's state plan and release the federal funds available under PL 94-142 unless the statutory provisions were agreed to in the plan.

We went a few rounds, with Ambach getting increasingly irritated at my intransigence. Eventually, with the concurrence of the state Board of Regents, New York submitted a plan that Tom Irvin and BEH staff felt met the provision.

New York officials sometimes said that their system was still intact, just with a new level of review. No challenge reached the courts to my knowledge, so I assume New York did, in fact, comply with the statute. As was our practice, we did not publicize the resolution of such disputes in the media, although we made the information about the decision available to anyone as it was a part of the public record. Parents, for example, often were following the deliberations carefully.

Texas

We had a similar negotiation with Texas. Once again, the issue was the authority of the state board of education and the Commissioner to resolve appeals from special education hearings. I recall Commissioner M. L. Brockette saying to me, "Ed, the Board will eat my lunch if I go along with this." I am not sure what gustatory events transpired, but the plan was eventually signed.

Missouri

Missouri presented a different case, though just as difficult. PL 94-142 had a provision that required children in non-public schools to be able to participate, proportionately, in the programs supported by the Act. That did not mean that money would flow to the private or parochial schools. (This was in the days when we still had a clear Constitutional separation between state and church.) One possible solution was to offer programs on public school grounds, which children from private schools might attend. That pattern was, supposedly, in place already under the provisions of Title I of the Elementary and Secondary Education Act passed 10 years earlier. The statutory language was, as I recall, identical.

But Missouri had a state constitution and laws that strictly separated public funds and private schools. Its officials felt compliance with 94-142 was impossible, and their state plan did not include the needed provision.

We held a series of discussions with them: I met with State Commissioner Arthur Mallory personally, and BEH staff convened with other Missouri officials many times. This was a situation full of nuance, gray areas and a wish to see the funds flow to assist Missouri's children. (True in the instances in other states as well, of course.)

Fortunately, we also had some history with the Office of Education approving other state plans from Missouri under similar statutes. Somehow language was crafted that circumvented the objections of its officials. At the point where our staff and attorneys thought we had a deal, I called it "The

Missouri Compromise," and we moved on. As the saying goes for legislation and sausage making, "One does not want to watch it too closely."

California

The most dramatic confrontation over PL 94-142 came in California with Wilson Riles, the Chief State School Officer. Under the Related Services provisions of the Act, if a local school staff developed an IEP for a child with physical disabilities and included physical or occupational therapy, the school district and/or the state education agency had to provide that service.

Riles, an elected official, took the position that in California, physical and occupational therapy were provided by another state agency, usually the Health Department. In some instances that department did not have services available to meet the IEP requirements for certain children because of budgetary limitations. Parents, correctly, objected to that failure to provide services and contacted a public interest law firm associated with the Center for Independent Living in Berkeley, which, in turn, contacted us.

Riles sent his deputy to argue with us, while commenting about us in the press in a negative fashion. Although the deputy came with "an attitude," in modern parlance, BEH staff and I met with him at length and tried to convince him that there was no give in the Act. The children had to have the services and, if necessary, California would have to use its federal or state funds to supply them.

Eventually Riles came to Washington and denounced me to a press gathering on the Capitol steps. It may have received good coverage in California, but in battle-hardened Washington, he would have had to immolate himself to get attention. Jousting with bureaucrats was minor league activity. Riles did lobby the California delegation and got some responses from a few more conservative members. Their inquiries were, it seemed to us, pro forma, and when we explained the law and our position, none pressed us further.

The amount of funds involved was impressive. I was withholding about $90 million, so the stakes were quite high. California Members of Congress who had supported the law, such as Senator Alan Cranston (Democrat, CA), and a number of Representatives—I recall George Armitage Miller (Democrat, CA) as one—followed the issue closely but were willing to uphold the law without interference. I respected them. I am not sure how Commissioner Riles felt. Of particular importance, legislatively, was Senator Alan Cranston. Cranston was on the Education Subcommittee and naturally was "a player" in such issues. I spoke with a top legislative aide and explained our position and why we felt Commissioner Riles was showboating. The aide reviewed the matter and said he had no further questions.

California finally signed the plan.

At some point, Riles was rumored to be a candidate for another elective office, but I don't recall his running successfully. I would like to say that it was his just deserts, but that may just be my own conceit.

Mississippi

Mississippi shared with every state a common failure to educate its children with disabilities. As a poor state, it truly had a substandard program of services, although there certainly were willing and effective teachers working with some children—just not enough. There was also considerable precedent of resistance to providing and paying for the needed and required services to children.

Because of the pattern of failure in Mississippi, the Children's Defense Fund (CDF), a Washington-based advocacy agency, filed suit against the state education agency for non-compliance with their own state plan and therefore, PL 94-142.

The CDF was founded and headed by the highly respected Marian Wright Edelman. She was a native South Carolinian who had attended Spellman College and Yale Law School. She was the first Black woman to pass the Mississippi Bar. Recognized as a Civil Rights leader, she later was named a McArthur "Genius Award" fellow.

The attorney pursuing the case for CDF was Dan Yohalem. Bright, dedicated and arrogant, he knew he was working for a powerhouse and expected "bureaucrats" to roll over to his demands. We had many meetings with him, discussing the issues and taking steps that seemed appropriate to remedy problems, but, as it turned out, we did not do all that he, Edelman and the CDF had in mind.

While the case was in process, the CDF wanted us to cut off funding to Mississippi. While that action may have bolstered its legal strategy, it is not how government education funding works. A state plan is, under the law, a statement of assurances. Assuming all of the appropriate assurances are included in the document, it has to be approved even if the agency is doubtful that the state will really fulfill the plan. If it doesn't, a complaint leads to an examination—in this case by BEH staff—and a solution is sought. If there is no solution, the next allotment of funds under the act can be halted, as in the California case mentioned earlier. In many states the annual review of the state plan would result in our staff extracting new assurances of services; those changes were gradually implemented so that the nation was moving forward toward compliance.

As we saw BEH's role, it was to make the program work and to get the assurances and changes necessary to allow the funds to flow. CDF wanted us to be more like the Office of Civil Rights, that is, a compliance agency, staffed by attorneys who conduct investigations, make findings, sometimes establish numerical quotas and cut off funds if necessary. While we both reached the same conclusions, we approached it as special educators trying to make it work, not as confrontational lawyers, Our process, dictated by the law as we saw it, was to get the processes changed and move ahead.

When Mississippi officials made promises to us, in writing, that they would correct the issues in dispute, if we found their assurances reasonable and not frivolous, we agreed to the funding under the law. In BEH's view, that kind of year-by-year examination and resubmission by all of the states leading to approval of funding was part and parcel of moving the Act successfully toward its objectives.

Although we did not know it at the time, CDF's leader, Marian Wright Edelman, saw us a derelict in our duty and was very angry about it. In effect, she wanted BEH to either win the suit or make it moot by finding the state out of compliance and cutting off the funds.

Edelman apparently had a long memory and knew how to bear a grudge; this brought me some pain down the road, but more of that later.

New Mexico

These were not the only states where early problems had to be overcome. New Mexico declined to participate at all. It later lost a federal court suit for failing to meet the anti-discrimination standard of Section 504, or the Rehabilitation Act, and was ordered to essentially comply with PL 94-142 without getting the federal money. It ultimately sent in a state plan about two years later and began to receive funding.

Colorado

Resistance had to be overcome in Colorado as well. There legislators expressed fears about early childhood education and IEPs calling for "snowmobiles" to ferry disabled children to and from school in the winter. I met with state legislators at the request of State Commissioner Cal Frazier. Sure enough, one legislator asked me what would happen if an IEP called for a snowmobile for some child. I told him the IEP would be developed by teachers and administrators in Colorado schools without any federal input, and that prospect seemed unlikely. I also clarified that children under five did not have to be educated under the law, although it was encouraged and federal funds could be spent for that purpose if Colorado's school officials wished. Colorado agreed and we moved ahead.

Progress in Implementation

Considering the complexity of PL 94-142 and the historic changes in school practice that were involved, overall the evolution of the act into national law was surprisingly smooth.

The primary problems that state and local officials reported involved implementing the IEP provisions. Many places developed elaborate procedures. One I saw was 30 pages in length and, of course, the problems were blamed on the "feds." We spent a lot of time, most of it fruitless, trying to help people understand the federal requirements were quite simple and that however good the intentions, the elaborations were from their own states or districts. I know I was asked about those provisions every year that I spoke at the national convention of the Council for Exceptional Children.

Parents complained about the slowness in "finding" children in need of special education and about the failure to provide full services. Districts complained about the impartial hearings that were necessary and the occasional court suits. The stories usually involved hundreds of thousands of dollars spent on legal fees defending against an unjustified demand for services by a parent.

But the overall picture was positive. Children and their parents had leverage in the system—a great contrast from the days when they could simply be turned away without recourse. As for the hearings and court cases, they were miniscule considering that within a few years of its enactment, PL 94-142 was assisting in educating more than five million children. Court cases in a year were something like one in a million, however disturbing they might be to the people directly involved. Hearings occurred more frequently, but probably no more than one per 100,000 children.

While the funding formula called for the potential maximum appropriations, each year the President's Office of Management and Budget and Congress worked their will, providing increases well short of the authorization. Still, hundreds of millions of dollars flowed to the state and local educational agencies in the first year and increased each subsequent year—a huge difference compared with the sums fewer than $50 million that were reached after the first five years of the Carey Bill, (Title VI).

During the years between 1975 when the act was signed, 1978 when its provisions had to be in place, and 1981 when the Reagan Administration began, the professional staff of BEH held hundreds of meetings with parents, state and local officials, and others to smooth the implementation of the law. Over that period, despite inevitable problems, there never was a time when there was a public outcry because people affected by the law did not feel that it was a force for good, or that those administering it weren't acting in good faith. For those who think all government is bad, that is a lesson to be learned.

CHAPTER 15

The Carter Administration and Beyond

The four years of the Carter presidency, 1976 to 1980, were a busy time. Under the newly appointed Secretary of HEW, Joseph Califano, we moved ahead implementing PL 94-142, negotiating participation by the states as detailed in the previous chapter. We also brought about Captioned Television for the Deaf on the national networks, something Califano told me brought him great satisfaction. It was a tiny item in the massive HEW program complex, but it had a real impact on the lives of persons who were deaf.

In 1979 the Department of Education was established by law in accord with President Carter's proposal. Califano and other supporters of HEW opposed the creation of the new department, but Congress ultimately agreed with the President. Interestingly, Muriel Humphrey, wife of former Vice President Hubert Humphrey, was serving in the Senate, and she became the prime sponsor of the Department legislation—a wise political move by the leadership, blunting the opposition to a degree.

The Road to Being Named Assistant Secretary

As the director of BEH since 1969, I was identified by many people and organizations as the "point person" for advocacy for education of children with disabilities. Many organizations had been kind enough to recognize me with awards, and so there was support for me in the Nixon, Ford and Carter Administrations to continue in my leadership role.

From 1973 to 1975, the Nixon and Ford Administrations decided to change the position of Bureau Chief in the Office of Education to a Schedule C position. Schedule C positions were presidential appointments and not covered by civil service criteria or tenure protections. In practice, they are made at the department level, not by the President, but cleared by the White House. There are hundreds, perhaps thousands, of such appointments, and they can range across grade levels from middle to top levels. Above these departmental positions are sub-cabinet appointments—assistant, deputy and under-secretaries, and the secretaries themselves—all the result of nominations by the President and subject to confirmation by the Senate.

I was under no particular pressure to take a Schedule C appointment while Sid Marland and later, Ted Bell, were Commissioners and I was working on PL 94-142. I was not on the favored list of the political cadre in HEW and the Office of Education, however, because of my work with Congress on developing that bill, which the Nixon Administration opposed, and my strong Congressional ties with staff and some committee members.

John Ottina, for example, served as Assistant Commissioner for Administration in OE. A non-educator with a business background, he was a Nixon loyalist and made clear that I was not on his favorite persons list. But other than my fighting for increased sums for the education of the handicapped programs, we had no personal clashes.

During this time my official title was Acting Deputy Commissioner, and I remained director of the Bureau of Education for the Handicapped. I chose not to take the Schedule C position because I did not want to be a presidential appointee under Richard Nixon. I also felt I would be vulnerable to firing for political reasons without the civil service protections.

About the time Gerald Ford assumed the presidency, Bell left OE to return to Utah and Ottina became Commissioner. He soon pressured me to take the Schedule C, or he would appoint someone else.

Fortunately, Fred Weintraub of CEC and other friends among the disability community brought this to the attention of the Congressional supporters of the Bureau, of special education and of me. One interesting tactic that I believe Weintraub came up with was to remind the Administration and both Republican and Democratic members of Congress of the time E. Howard Hunt had been arrested because of the Watergate break-in and asked for "discrete reprisals" against me and my assistant, Harvey Liebergott. The disability community asked if this were a "discrete reprisal."

During this time I got a phone call from Representative Albert Quie, the senior Republican on the House Education Committee. I had always found him to be a straight shooter, respected by Democrats and Republicans alike. Quie reassured me that as long as he was in the House, the Administration would never fire me (I assume he meant without good cause). I told him I appreciated that very much, and explained my basic reason for refusing the position was that as Watergate unfolded, I just could not serve as a Nixon presidential appointee. He respected my concerns, and that was the last I heard of being forced into Schedule C.

Joe Califano Becomes Secretary of HEW Under President Carter

In 1977, as the Carter Administration began filling its jobs, I became aware that I had not been contacted by the HEW Secretary's office. I was still a professional appointment in the civil service and kept my "acting" title. People began asking about it, perhaps again on "the Hill," but not directly to me.

Eventually I got a call to see Secretary Califano. When I arrived at his office, he seemed reserved in his approach—there were no, "Well, you fought the good fight, welcome aboard" type remarks. Instead, he asked, "How long have you been here?" I explained I had been appointed in 1967 under President Johnson, but as a civil servant. He commented that was about 10 years, and he thought people usually wanted to change jobs every seven years or so. I replied that I considered mine an unusual job. First, I had helped Congress create the Bureau, served as Deputy Associate

Commissioner, and then two years later, as Associate Commissioner. It occurred to me that that appointment, which happened in the early days of the Nixon Administration, may have been something he wondered about. Actually, I was the choice of then Commissioner Jim Allen, a liberal Republican on social policy, who was later fired for questioning the Cambodian incursion in remarks on a college campus.

I told the Secretary that the Bureau had been growing while I was there, including, most recently, during the passage of PL 94-142, and I was now looking forward to putting that legislation into place and implementing it. For me, the job was constantly changing, not the same job at all. Further, I was a specialist in disability, not a general administrator, so this was part of my career choice.

He responded somewhat frostily that "everyone" was telling him to appoint me, including Republicans (probably Al Quie, or perhaps Senator Stafford or Senator Javits, all of whom I had worked cooperatively with under the Republicans), and also mentioned former Secretary Wilbur Cohen, then the Dean of Education at the University of Michigan. Cohen, as noted earlier, was an architect of Medicare, working with Ways and Means Chairman Wilbur Mills, and I could not have thought of any better referral source. I told Califano I admired Wilbur Cohen very much. When he and I had talked about my hopes for 94-142, he had given me advice about taking and incorporating a piece at a time and then coming back for more the next chance I got.

After that Califano warmed noticeably and I knew I could relax. He did insist I take the Schedule C appointment, and I did, reluctantly. Having turned down a number of outside and inside government positions, I wanted to develop PL 94-142, and I would take my chances on no tenure.

My reluctance was not just a matter of politics. Earlier in my career, I had been under pressure to make program choices that I refused, e.g., releasing the Julie Nixon film, and a grant to Louisiana, supposedly to help secure Senator Russell Long's support for Nixon. Had I been a Schedule C then, I would have been "history" in a minute. I thought then and think now that program officials who sign off on grants ought to be in the civil service, and that their being fired should become public and has to be for good cause.

I mentioned to Califano that when I was appointed to the civil service as a "supergrade," which was one of the top three grades of the civil service ladder at the time (GS 16, 17 and 18), Marvin Watson, an assistant to LBJ, had invited all the new, non-political appointees to the White House and showed us around. It was an exciting event, and a few days later I received an 8 x 10 color, signed photograph of the President (no doubt, by auto-pen). That first Christmas we all were invited again to a little reception—cookies, punch, etc.—and began to receive Christmas cards from the President and Lady Bird, Marvin, and Ben Barnes, later Speaker of the House in the Texas legislature. I am not sure about the Barnes tie; I never met him or had any professional contact with him, but maybe he was casting bread on the political waters.

I told Califano I kept Johnson's picture and one of JFK up in my office throughout the Nixon years. He liked the story, it seems, and before long, each top appointee in HEW received a picture of Secretary Califano.

A Sit-in at HEW

Sections 503 and 504 of the Rehabilitation Act, outlawing discrimination against people with disabilities, had been passed by Congress in 1973. It was now 1976 and the regulations to guide the government and the public had never been written and promulgated. Of course, this delay was under the Nixon and Ford Administrations, but with the new Carter Administration in power, activists in the Disability Rights movement decided to draw public attention to this failing. They organized a sit-in, or perhaps more precisely, a wheel chair roll-in demonstration in the entrance hall of the HEW building, calling for the regulations to be developed and implemented.

Secretary Califano called me and he was furious. We just got in office he said, essentially, why are they protesting now? Where were they when

Nixon and Ford were in power? He wanted me to speak to the protestors and reason with them. I had not known of the plans for the protest, but said I would go, and suggested the general counsel of some other responsible representative should assure them the Secretary was committed to getting the regulations into effect. "They are your people," he said forcibly, "you handle it."

The disability group leaders wanted to be sure they had Califano's attention, and we did our best to assure them we were already beginning work on the regulations. The fact that the working group from across the disability-related programs in HEW was headed by the general counsel, Peter Libassi sent a positive message. I remember a day when we invited disabled people and parents to tell their stories to the working group. A woman from rural West Virginia told her story.

She had a daughter with mild mental retardation who had no placement in school. Each day the school bus stopped at the base of their driveway and picked up a group of children. She said her daughter would cry and say, "Mommy, why can't I go to school?" As she told the story, tears came to her eyes, and to mine. When I looked across the table and saw tears in Peter Libassi's eyes, I knew the regulations were on a fast track. I later learned that Libassi had a daughter with a disability; he understood all too well the problems people faced with getting appropriate schooling.

The Confirmation Process

As with my appointment to head the Bureau in the past, "the field," i.e., the special education community, was pleased. There was a general feeling that I would be a good candidate for appointment as the first Assistant Secretary for the Office of Special Education and Rehabilitative Services (OSERS). A careerist appointed as Assistant Secretary was rare, except in the State Department, where Ambassadors were sometimes nominated for such posts. More often than not, nominees had little experience in the administration of complex programs and had limited success in providing leadership for the federal agencies, involved and to the field in general.

I knew a good bit about the backstage workings of government both in the White House and on Capitol Hill, but I had no experience in the confirmation process. Richard I. Beattie, a topflight New York lawyer and a graduate of Dartmouth College and University of Pennsylvania Law School who was working in HEW at the time was tapped to help shepherd me and other new ED leaders through the process.

Joe Califano, then Secretary of HEW, had invited Beattie to Washington. Like many others, including Califano himself, he had walked away from a lucrative law practice to serve in the government. Beattie specialized in corporate law and was an early participant in "leveraged buyouts." and other merger and acquisition activities. He had had a successful and well compensated career already, and his government service was not a stepping stone to a related or lobbying job in the private sector. (In 2006, he was named by a European business magazine as the "World's Leading Merger and Acquisition Attorney.") As chairman of the prestigious New York law firm Simpson Thacher & Bartlett, he began a foundation with his own funds to improve public education in New York City schools. He also headed a commission appointed by Mayor Ed Koch in the 1980s to review and improve special education in the city, on which I was happy to serve.

Beattie left being general counsel at HEW at the request of the Carter White House to take on the assignment of counsel and director of the transition to the new Department of Education. He advised on setting up the structure, recruiting top officials and, in my case, helping me get over some serious hurdles on the way to nomination by the President and confirmation by the Senate. The task of structuring and helping select staff for the new department was an awesome responsibility. He also had taken himself out of the running for a position in ED.

He and I had met when Califano asked him to help me work through the maze of legal steps necessary for us to secure captioning of television for deaf persons. Beattie and his assistants were invaluable since the Office of Education and HEW had little if any experience working with the private sector, having dealt almost exclusively with grants to non-profit agencies until then.

When the decisions I made regarding closed captioning were later questioned by OE contracting staff, who reported them quietly to the subcommittee of the House of Representatives headed by a loose cannon, Representative H. L. Fountain (Democrat, NC), the strength of the legal analysis Beattie and his staff had provided quickly resolved any issues. I told a staff member from the Fountain committee that if it came to hearings, his boss and fellow representatives would find out that some of the top lawyers in the country had been involved in every step we had taken. I never heard from them again.

In the midst of the process of being nominated by the President, Dick called me one day to tell me that Marian Wright Edelman was suggesting her opposition to my appointment along with a group in her orbit, the Disability Rights Legal Defense Fund (DRLDF), based on her disagreement with how I had handled the implementation of PL 94-142 in Mississippi. I was really taken aback. Everything I had heard at that point about Edelman was positive—she was an icon to various foundations. To my knowledge, we at the Bureau had no conflicts with the people at DRLDF. A group close to them had, in fact, asked me for help in the California state plan process, and we had worked with them to a successful conclusion.

The issue in Mississippi involved a suit by her Children's Defense Fund against the State of Mississippi for failing to provide appropriate services to children with disabilities. A lawyer working for CDF, Dan Yohalem, had met with the Bureau staff and with me, urging us to cut off funding for Mississippi, thereby strengthening their suit, or making it moot. Our position was that the statute we were operating under, PL 94-142, was structured so that assurances from a state were appropriate responses to negative findings, and we, of course, had to monitor to see that the assurances were met. A cut off of funds, would, of course, hurt all the children in Mississippi who were benefiting from the funds. Our position was that we wanted to help the existing children and make improvements where there were programmatic shortfalls. Edelman and Yohalem wanted us to act like the HEW Office of Civil Rights, move in with attorneys, set numerical goals for services, etc. This alternative way of enforcing was possible because OCR had a different legislative mission. In fact, OCR could have pursued Mississippi for discriminating against children with disabilities under the provisions of Sections 503 and 504 of the Rehabilitation Act of 1973. Why CDF did not follow that route is unknown to me, but during this time the Republican Administration was in place, just before the Carter election.

Beattie suggested I ask for a meeting with Edelman and try to resolve the issues she had with me. He set it up. I learned from him that Edelman found my discussion of the Mississippi proceedings inadequate, and I suspected as much when she lectured me about my proper role and responsibilities, suggesting quotas and numerical measurements similar to those the Office of Civil Rights might use. Although no harsh words were spoken, it was also clear that my 14 years of advocacy for the programs CDF had so lately discovered did not sway her negative view of my appointment, nor did Peggy's and my work in the Civil Rights movement in Alabama (which I did not mention).

Fortunately, my track record attracted many supporters. Every major parent group and professional association, and key Members of Congress from both parties, supported my appointment. I understand there was some wavering in the White House given Edelman's prestige and President Carter's and Vice-President Mondale's commitment to Civil Rights, but my record in Washington and my earlier involvement in Civil Rights activities in Alabama probably helped. I know that Beattie's support was also critical when the Administration was reconsidering my appointment, although he would never suggest anything of the sort. In any case, the President nominated me and the Senate confirmed me unanimously after a careful review of my finances and other FBI checks and a non-challenging hearing. Although the presidential proclamation identified me as a citizen of Virginia, I asked Senator Jacob Javits, Republican of New York, to introduce me to the Senate hearing; and at, I am sure, Roy Millenson's recommendation, he did so, establishing again a non-partisan approach to the job.

Edelman continues to be revered and has generally been a force for good. Later, I did see her publicly turn against two members of Congress, George Armitage Miller (Democrat, CA) and Thomas J. Downey (Democrat, NY), both long-time supporters of causes in which they all shared interests. They had, in fact, sponsored the child development legislation she favored, but fell out of favor because they did not agree precisely with her views on specifics. I felt she had succumbed to the hubris that many who gain power have; she began to think her views were infallible and that anyone who disagreed with her must be punished.

With President Carter celebrating
the new Department of Education

Subsequent Developments

My pleasure at being Assistant Secretary was relatively short-lived—it was about a year before the 1980 election. Ironically, around that time I was contacted by the civil service and told of a new program for people like me, career professionals who were appointed to political positions. A new corps, the Senior Executive Service, had been established to make sure people with those qualifications were not lost every time an Administration changed. So I would be eligible for a senior executive position when my presidential appointment ended. I would not be guaranteed the same position I held, but would be eligible for a senior position at the same level in any governmental agency.

During that time, I was responsible not just for the Bureau, which had been renamed the Office of Special Education Programs (OSEP), but also for the Rehabilitation Services Administration (RSA), which had been led earlier by the icon of rehabilitation, Mary Switzer, and for the National Institute of Disability Research (NIDR). That agency had earlier been poorly named the National Institute for Handicapped Research, which drew a number of jibes.

The Assistant Secretary's Office was called the Office of Special Education and Rehabilitative Services (OSERS). This multi-billion-dollar agency had several hundred employees, including 10 regional RSA offices, and represented a much larger sphere of control than I had experienced in directing the Bureau. I had to put in place an Office of the Assistant Secretary, as well as fill a number of key appointments, including the Commissioner of Rehabilitation and the director of NIDR.

I called upon my key associates Bob Herman, who was named Deputy Assistant Secretary, and Doris Gamser, who headed the Executive Secretariat, to essentially control the communication among the programs themselves, and among the Office, Congress and the public.

Moving quickly to establish a structure, we depended a great deal on the key professionals in each of the agencies. It was my belief that operating a large and highly individualized grant program in three agencies did not lend itself to a single executive making all decisions.

RSA was an "old-line" agency compared to OSEP. It had existed for many years and suffered from entrenched bureaucracies. BEH during my tenure had grown from about 20 people to just under 200, and virtually all were professionals committed to disability, not general government administrators. NIDR was, for the most part, composed of administrators who had been in RSA until the Institute was created.

Had President Carter been reelected, I would have hoped to make it a stronger research agency staffed by scientists, in the model of the National Institutes of Health.

The Reagan Years

The new Reagan Administration was very rigid about the conservative bona fides of its appointees. It shunned even moderate East Coast Republicans, like Christopher Cross, counsel to the Republicans on the Education Committee in the House, who was passed over for a position in ED despite excellent qualifications.

I could have had an executive position in the government and perhaps even have headed the Office of Special Education Programs (part of OSERS—the original BEH). The incoming Secretary, Ted Bell, my old colleague, had raised that possibility, although he did not specifically offer me the position. I told him that I felt the time was right for me to leave Washington. It was clear to me that I could not, even as a civil servant, work comfortably in the Reagan Administration. It would not be fair to an elected President, and I joked that I would surely become clinically depressed (in fact, that happened to one of my colleagues from BEH days).

When word began to circulate that I was leaving, I had a very nice phone call from Senator Robert Stafford, a Republican. He said he was sorry to learn I was leaving and asked if it was because the incoming

President had threatened to end the Department of Education and repeal PL 94-142. He said that, if so, I should not worry, because as chairman of the Senate Education Subcommittee, he was not going to introduce such legislation for the Administration, even as a courtesy. I thanked him, most sincerely, but told him I thought I would not feel it was appropriate for me to stay. For those familiar with today's blind political loyalties, the days of moderates in the Congress who voted their beliefs, not the party doctrine, must seem quaint.

Meanwhile, I watched OSERS under Reagan with interest, and sometimes dismay. The first person appointed in my old position of Assistant Secretary was Jean Tufts, a kindly lady from New Hampshire, who was most identified with the National School Boards Association, but had only a limited background in local disability programs in her home state. Her husband was a leader in the New Hampshire Senate.

She did her best to do a credible job, but unfortunately died in February, 1983 after a long illness.

At the time Mrs. Tufts was nominated Assistant Secretary, the Reagan Administration was stuffing right wing, conservative "Christians" into the Department of Education, paying back the organizations which had backed him. One such appointee to a policy position advising the Secretary was a woman who opined publicly that she had doubts about the department's disability programs, since "God had created them disabled and we should not interfere with his work." That was too much for the Education leaders in Congress, and she soon disappeared from view, perhaps to a quiet spot in another agency.

Following Mrs. Tufts, the President, once again insisting on a politically correct background, appointed Madeline Will, who was married at the time to conservative columnist George Will, and was the mother of a young boy with Down Syndrome. Coincidentally, she had written to me when the Wills moved to the D.C. area, asking about programs for young children with Down Syndrome, and I was able to refer her to a preschool program we had funded in Montgomery County, Maryland—a rarity in those days.

Mrs. Will had a strong interest in "mainstreaming" and also in employment programs, and she was an effective advocate for those ideas. While "mainstreaming" had been a special education concept since the 1960s, it got a great deal of new visibility through her efforts. But she had never held an administrative position before, and it was felt that running a multi-billion-dollar agency was not something she was prepared for.

Later in the Reagan years, Dr. Robert Davila was appointed Assistant Secretary. To me it seemed that he was the most qualified of the Reagan appointees. A deaf man, he had earned a doctorate, taught at Gallaudet University for the Deaf in Washington and became a dean there. He was intelligent and hard-working, and well-liked by colleagues.

It was on the program side that the Reagan Administration was up to no good.

The Reagan Administration Attempts to Weaken the Act's Protections

As self-proclaimed critic of "big government," Ronald Reagan was no fan of what we had achieved. During his presidential campaign, he had said he wanted to repeal not only the Education of All Handicapped Children Act, PL 94-142, as well as the provisions of the Rehabilitation Act that prohibited discrimination against persons with disabilities in programs receiving federal funds. He wanted to abolish the Department of Education altogether.

Sections 503 and 504 of the Rehabilitation Act offered key protections to people with disabilities in education, employment, health, housing, transportation and other federally funded programs. They were the forerunners for today's Americans With Disabilities Act, which expanded the protections for people with disabilities beyond those covering only federally funded or assisted programs as under the Rehabilitation Act.

As President, Reagan found that Congress did not support his plan for repealing the disability provisions or for terminating the Department of Education, so his Administration decided to change (in fact, substantially weaken) the regulations determining compliance with the Act.

The proposed revision to the PL 94-142 regulations created a furor among parents of children with disabilities and advocacy groups, and they turned for assistance to Senator Lowell Weicker, chairman of the Disability Policy Subcommittee, which was the descendent of the Randolph subcommittee on the handicapped. The subcommittee had jurisdiction for federal special education and rehabilitation programs.

Although a Republican, Weicker was outspoken in his criticism of the White House for its regulation proposals and promised to reverse them in the law if necessary. He was a maverick by inclination and the parent of a child with a disability. Needless to say, the Reagan Administration did not look kindly on his efforts. Later, Weicker ran as an independent for the Governorship of Connecticut and won.

The proposed changes in the regulations were drafted by the Office of Special Education Programs (OSEP)—the new title for BEH. It was headed at that time by Dr. Edward Sontag. who advocated for the new regulations in public speeches across the nation and in meetings with the Council for Exceptional Children and other advocacy groups.

One evening during this time we shared an airplane ride to Washington. We had become colleagues over the years. He had begun his federal career in BEH as an intern from Professor Dan Sage of Syracuse University's public administration program and I hired him afterward (in part because there was a "hiring freeze" which prevented us from hiring people not already in the government). During the flight we discussed his role in these regulations, which I found abhorrent and assumed he did also, although I should have remembered his "negative" involvement in the Maryland court case which required my testimony to rectify.

I understood that, as a career civil servant heading OSEP, he had to explain the Administration's position, but he was not required to advocate for it (or, conversely, provide opposing proposals). His was not a political or policy position that served at the pleasure of the President, and I suggested that he play a less aggressive role in supporting the changes.

I was under the impression that he agreed, but to my surprise he continued to urge the approval of the regulations, causing him to be seen as a traitor (or perhaps a slightly less negative term) by many special educators, including old friends and colleagues. Sontag later worked in several capacities in Republican Administrations, and a number of people I talked to felt that his actions were based on his ambition to get choice political appointments.

At the time, I also was disappointed by the behavior of CEC, the National Association for Retarded Citizens (NARC), and certain other groups who for many years had consistently and effectively advocated for children and adults with disabilities. They indicated support for continued discussions with Sontag and the Administration on regulatory revisions even though they could have, and should have, refused to even consider such changes.

I called Fred Weintraub, my old friend and colleague, who was still director of legislative affairs for the CEC and Paul Marchand, the executive director of NARC (now The Arc) and also the coalition that brought together different organizations to work on disability issues. I asked why they were following that course of action and tried to convince them to change their approach

Weintraub and Marchand both said they were trying to keep the channels of communication open. They feared that total opposition would cut them off from access in an Administration that demanded compliance with its views. The Reagan team, in contrast to earlier Republican and Democratic Administrations, took a "no holds barred" approach to any dissent by anyone in either party.

I felt that they were undercutting Senator Weicker (although they had no intention of doing that), since the Senator had earned the Administration's ire (more so because he was a Republican) by adamantly opposing its policies. The willingness of groups like CEC, NARC and the coalition of disability-interested groups to keep discussing the issue, could be thrown in his face by the Reagan White House. I found that a number of other special education colleagues had similar concerns, and after a good number of "feedback" calls, CEC and the others changed their course.

After a torrent of public complaints, estimated in the tens of thousands, Education Secretary Terrence Bell announced that the proposed regulations had been withdrawn. It was clear the White House felt it would lose the public relations battle, and didn't have the votes if it came to Congressional action.

The Big Picture

That fruitless attempt by the Reagan Administration is instructive in a more general sense. Congress writes a law with a given intent. If an Administration—usually representing the opposition party—finds the provisions incompatible with its political or philosophical beliefs and, unwilling or unable to ask Congress to repeal or amend the legislation, it may decide to modify the regulations for the same purpose. Theoretically this should not be possible, since the regulations are to implement the act and be faithful to its intentions as passed by Congress and signed by the President.

A new twist on that theme was the position of President George W. Bush to define his understanding (or wishes) concerning the law through a statement when he signed the legislation. The Bush Administration held that such statements of intent have legal standing, and the Obama Administration, surprisingly, has continued the practice in a few instances. While there have been some vigorous objections in Congress, as there have been about a number of executive decisions which some members feel violate the Constitutional separation of powers, the courts have not dealt with this issue as I write.

There are many areas where compliance with an act's provisions may require regulations, and there is often considerable latitude to make those regulations more precise or more abstract. There have been a number of instances in the environmental area where Administrations, particularly under Reagan and Bush II, have weakened provisions, for example, allowing roads to be built in wilderness areas, approving logging, etc.

This can be done because some provisions don't specifically disallow such actions and permit some flexibility in interpretation, such as appropriate uses for national forests or parks. Sometimes these versions are challenged in the courts, and decisions have gone both ways, for and against the revised regulations.

CHAPTER 16

Post Government Work

Although I left the government, I did not leave behind my interest in advocacy for children and adults with disabilities.

After leaving Washington, I completed my third semester teaching public policy at the Harvard Graduate School of Education (HGSE), at an almost leisurely pace. I had been flying to Boston, teaching the seminar on Fridays and then returning to Washington. I used my leave days and, as I never took enough vacation (perhaps because of what my mentor Ollie Backus at Alabama called a "Jehovah Complex"—feeling one is indispensable at all times), I always had the maximum allowable in my account, unused.

The three spring semesters I taught at HGSE were a very rewarding time for me. The classes consisted of graduate students, almost all of them young professionals pursuing their Master's degrees. A number came from Professor Jeanne Chall's excellent reading program, Including Sally Grimes and Joan Sedita, both of whom are leaders in Massachusetts and nationally in training teachers to improve reading. There were also some doctoral students in Child Development or Social Policy and Administration sprinkled in. They all were bright and brought their own dedication to education to the seminar. What I was able to offer them was an inside view of public policy and education, with a particular focus on special education.

In many ways, the content paralleled this book. If I were teaching the course today, I would use it for supplemental reading, if not a required text. We were also able to discuss a number of events and concepts in "real time," as I shared the processes then underway, such as negotiating with state education officials, developing regulations, petitioning the Office of Management and Budget (OMB) and the House and Senate Appropriations Committees for funding, etc.

A number of students, including Grimes and Sedita, carried their interests into political activism and educational leadership at their local school boards, state education agencies and operating schools and school districts, and I loved hearing about their activities in the ensuing years as they made real contributions to children and to education.

It was not always fun that final spring. I intended to write a book like this, but the Reagan election cast a pall over my enthusiasm. I felt that in many ways my values, and those of people I admired, including many students, had been rejected by the public. Reagan, with his pledge to repeal the Education Department, PL 94-142 and the Civil Rights sections of the Rehabilitation Act, was going to try to undo what I, my colleagues and lawmakers had spent 14 years putting together.

Following my exit from Washington, I spent only one more semester at Harvard. Instead, I decided to take the job of president and chief executive officer of a multi-faceted complex of non-profit agencies that served children and adults in New York State, then known as the Human Resources Center. I had been offered the opportunity for a professorship at Hunter College by Donna Shalala, whom I admired very much for her work in Washington during the Carter years (she later served for eight years as Secretary of Health and Human Services under President Clinton). I was very taken with some of the conversations I had with my friend Jim Gallagher, however. He had left Washington, D.C. to become the director of the Frank Porter Graham Child Development Center at the University of North Carolina. We talked about loving to teach, but needing more active program-building and administration after our years heading federal agencies, and so I declined, with appreciation, Donna's invitation.

Instead, I was looking forward to heading the Human Resources Center. (After we developed an expanded concept of research and services, the board changed the name to The National Center for Disability Services.)

The best known part of the Human Resources Center (now renamed the Henry Viscardi Center) was the Human Resources School (now the Henry Viscardi School). This was a preschool through 12th-grade school for children with physical disabilities, ranging from cerebral palsy to muscular dystrophy, spina-bifida and various other orthopedic and health disorders. The school was tuition-free and supported by the Department of Education in New York State, supplemented by our private fund-raising.

People knowing of my interest in having children educated with non-disabled peers wondered about my choice. There were two reasons it appealed to me. First, the children were referred to come there by school districts at the request of their parents. No one was exiled to the school. Second, the graduation rate for the school was higher than for the average school in the state, as a result of the enriched curriculum and dedicated staff. One thing I learned from talking with the students and parents was that integrated education was not always the best setting for a given child. A number of students told me of the isolation they felt being the only ones using wheelchairs in their schools. A frequent story from parents was that in the younger grades they could invite children over to play after school, but as the children became more grown up and headed off to the malls and social activities, the children in the wheelchairs were often left behind.

At this school every child had the opportunity to be involved in modified sports, clubs, student government, theater and more. When I walked through the school with visitors, a frequent comment was, "I was afraid it would be depressing, but instead the children seem to be having such a good time." The lesson was that the school provided the opportunity to participate, not sit on the sidelines; to achieve and belong, not be isolated. It moved me to write an article at one point, "Is Julliard a Segregated School?" which argued that the renowned program for the performing arts produced superior results by having actors, dancers and musicians interact only with their peers. At the same time, when children chose to go back to a local school, we encouraged it, offering transition assistance as we could and supporting their decision.

I had a long-range plan to increase the mobility between the school and the local districts, something which was happening more frequently before I retired in 1994. Second, I wanted to review the curriculum to be sure it was topflight, and I found that our teachers were eager to do the same. I also brought in Dr. Nick Anastasiow, then a professor at Hunter College, to work with the preschool teachers to improve that program, which was good, but not cutting edge. Nick was a nationally known expert who played an important role for BEH in providing technical assistance to our early childhood grantees.

My second interest at the Center was developing the opportunities for post-secondary education and employment. PL 94-142 had set the stage for children to finish school, and the program was encouraging "transitional" planning for those who graduated or left school for other reasons. At the time, there still was no real structure awaiting them in the "real" world.

The Center's original program was called Abilities, Inc. It was a workshop that primarily employed people with physical disabilities. It was not a "sheltered workshop," paying sub-minimal wage, but instead was designed to help adults with disabilities, including some who had returned from World War II, to be prepared to take on electronic and mechanical work. Many of the jobs were in defense industries like Grumman Aviation or in the New York Telephone Company.

While I valued Abilities, it seemed to me its days were drawing to an end. I felt that we should be developing a modern rehabilitation center focusing on emerging jobs instead. So we set out to attract industry support for developing new curricula, such as word-processing, data entry and later on, computer programming. IBM and Honeywell helped us with equipment and grants, as did UPS. Later we branched into training laboratory technologists with assistance from pharmaceutical companies like Warner Lambert.

We also expanded on an existing activity started by the Center's founder, Henry Viscardi, forming relationships with business and labor organizations. To make the program more meaningful to those supporters, we charged them a fee in exchange for technical assistance, training sessions, etc., designed to help them hire workers with disabilities. Its predecessor, the earlier Industry Labor Council, as it was known, was primarily a program in name only. It stimulated some gifts, but it didn't really have an action orientation.

Eventually the Industry Labor Council reached across the country from Grumman on Long Island to McDonnell Douglas in Saint Louis to Boeing in Seattle, as well as to Ryder Systems in Miami. Altogether there were about 100 members. The Building Trades union in New York City, the International Brotherhood of Electrical Workers, and the Communication Workers of America were among the labor members.

Joint efforts in these various companies, sometimes with cooperation from local rehabilitation programs, resulted in an increase of 400 workers placed in jobs in the early years to 4,000 placements a year. Our national conferences were well attended by human resource personnel who shared ideas and various projects.

Our staff applied for government grants from the U.S. Labor Department and from the Rehabilitation Services Administration (RSA). I never appeared before any of the government agencies, certainly not before those I had headed; nor did I allow my name to be highlighted in our applications. I discussed ideas with our staff, read some proposals and offered advice, but the successes of our grant applications came from the ideas, the staff and previous performance, not my insider involvement. I held to the values I had championed in Washington. Then I would never speak with people approaching the Bureau with grants about their proposals, nor allow anyone to treat me to lunch or dinner. From 2007 to 2010, as Mayor of Venice, Florida, I followed the same policy, paying my own way. The Executive Branch is quite careful in this regard, Congress and the legions of lobbyists are another story.

Dr. Craig Michaels, now at Queens College of the City University of New York, was particularly creative in developing programs for students with learning disabilities. He secured the cooperation of three community colleges to accept young people with learning disabilities and to hold them to the same standards they had for other students. The program included peer tutors and a staff that would explain the students' conditions to their professors. Staff members were available to speak with disabled students, and would be allowed to read questions on exams to them, if needed. With these minor modifications, the students who had been experiencing a high failure rate in math and reading placement exams went on to succeed at a higher rate than many non-disabled students. The colleges adopted the program for non-disabled students who scored poorly on their placement exams, and achieved success with them as well.

The Center was one of the first three in the nation to develop a Job Coaching program, in which a staff member accompanied a student on a job, helped assure the work would be completed and gradually turned over the full task. If a student could not succeed, there were no recriminations against the employer; we went to work to find a situation that would be a better fit. This approach more than doubled the number of students getting jobs.

We held a very popular annual fund-raiser, Sports Night, during which athletes came to the Center for a reception and dinner, posed for Polaroid pictures with the attendees and participated in often hilarious skits with the children from the school. John Dockery, former New York Jets football player, and one of the few Harvard graduates in the NFL, agreed to be the master of ceremonies; and Jo Jo Starbuck, an Olympic ice-skater, took on the task of writing the skits and also attracting athletes. They both were wonderful to work with.

Fred Wilpon, owner of the New York Mets baseball team, gave the Center a few years before duties as the chairman of the board at his alma mater, the University of Michigan, became too demanding. Wilpon mentioned that his sister, Iris Katz, was a volunteer at the school, working with children with disabilities. No one on the staff was aware of her background—she was known only as Iris. She joined the school board and then the Center's board. Her husband, Saul, who was partners with Wilpon, told me he would help behind the scenes, but this was Iris' baby.

I also asked my Washington friend, Dick Beattie, to join the board and help me get going. He was then the managing partner of Simpson Thacher & Bartlett, one of the top law firms in New York, and working 70 to 80 hours a week involved in the most complicated corporate business. He gave me his time to come out to Long Island and worked with me to solve some early problems, and then I released him, knowing it was simply not right for him to spend that kind of time out of kindness. He suggested I contact a senior partner in his firm, Rick Dicke, who lived on Long Island and whose wife had been a volunteer in our school before an illness had made that impossible. Rick Dicke also joined the Board and soon became the chairman. Together Dick and Rick recruited John McGillicudy, chairman of the bank Manufacturers Hanover, to be our Sports Night Honoree and lend his prodigious fund-raising assistance.

With such a caliber of people and a number of other leaders from Wall Street recruited by the board, the Sports Night dinner grew from a $225,000 event to one that raised more than $1 million annually, topping $2 million in 2011—all for children and adults with disabilities in the tuition-free school and rehab center, primarily supported by state funds supplemented by private donations.

As we developed our national programs and our leadership activities through government programs, I asked the Board to change the Center's name to the National Center for Disability Service. In the years after I retired, the emphasis became more local, and the Board chose to rename the program twice more, first to Abilities! and, in Novemeber 2012, to the Henry Viscardi Center.

JIMMY CARTER

June 20, 1991

To Dr. Edwin Martin

Rosalynn and I are pleased to join your friends and colleagues in congratulating you for ten years of fine and dedicated service to the National Center for Disability Services.

Since leaving The White House, Rosalynn and I have learned of your efforts to develop a wide range of new programs which have led the way to improving the quality of life for thousands of disabled people. It is fitting that your achievements are being recognized in such a meaningful and special way by your peers.

Rosalynn and I are grateful for your service to our country while I was president, and we send you our best wishes for continued success throughout the years to come.

Sincerely,

Jimmy Carter

Dr. Edwin W. Martin, Jr.
President and Chief Executive Officer
HUMAN RESOURCES SCHOOL
Albertson, New York 11507

Further Developments in PL 94-142

At the same time, in Washington, provisions were added to the law that provided that transitional planning should occur for students during their senior high school years. It was a major step forward. Dr. Susan Hasazi, now a professor at the University of Vermont, who worked with Senator Robert Stafford of Vermont, chairman of the Education Committee, did the key staff work on this provision. She was particularly interested in the transition from school to work—a key concept.

I met with Hasazi after I had left government service. As a professional and "alumnus" of "the Hill" and ED, I was advocating for funds to be used to develop a range of innovative programs for high school students with disabilities, as well as work-related programs, because special education for children past elementary school had serious problems. The models primarily used for younger children did not really fit adolescents, and yet more and more students were staying in school during their high school years. What would post-high school bring?

Hasazi was concerned that any other uses of funds available would dilute the much needed school-to-work emphasis and was reluctant to change. We could not agree on which should get priority, but our conversation was conducted in a friendly fashion. We recognized the merits of both approaches.

I found that staff members in the House were willing to develop a version of the bill including modifying some language. In the conference between the houses, the Senate language predominated, but there was legislative history in the "conference report," which supported a variety of secondary school innovations.

The impact of the school-to-work provision was very beneficial in orienting school programs more toward post-school activities. It was my experience that no one in the schools ever asked, "What are the children doing after school?" It was one way of partially evaluating the effectiveness of special education—not the specifics of instruction, but the goals and directions.

When I was at BEH, we had taken the first steps toward this evolution by sponsoring a conference that brought together, for the very first time, leaders from various states representing three programs: special education, vocational education and vocational rehabilitation. That conference recognized the problem that the transition provisions highlighted, but follow-up was inconsistent, and for the most part programs were not developed. The rehab people, for example, had no information about students who could and should become their clients after completing special education programs.

The Clinton and Bush Years

I did not follow closely the appointments during the Clinton years, other than that of a friend, Judy Heumann, who became Assistant Secretary. She had been a co-founder of the Berkeley Center for Independent Living, along with California director of Rehabilitation Services, Ed Roberts. The Independent Living Center movement was designed to offer service programs for people with disabilities, by people with disabilities—they both used wheelchairs.

The Assistant Secretaries appointed under President George W. Bush were not well known in the special education field, and the current education leaders with whom I spoke to at the time did not identify them with specific leadership activities. However, there were significant legislative programs passed that impacted students with disabilities. "No Child Left Behind" (NCLB) evolved from the Elementary and Secondary Education Act. There were also modifications of PL 94-142, including changing its title to "The Individuals with Disabilities Education Act" (IDEA).

IDEA importantly expanded federal education aid to programs for youngsters from ages 0 to 2 and 3 to 5. These programs did not have specific funding authorities previously, although some had been funded by the states under PL 94-142 and various "discretionary" programs, such as the provisions of The Education of the Handicapped Act that authorized the Secretary of Education to make grants to non-profit agencies, schools and states for early childhood programs. The new state grant programs, paralleling PL 94-142's primary emphasis on children of school age, brought new services to children and assisted in their development. As our early efforts with model programs had demonstrated, many children had less severe educational disadvantages as a result of the early "interventions."

NCLB, with its strong focus on testing, has been controversial, with strong advocates and detractors. As I have not been directly involved in educational programs under these acts, I cannot add further understanding as to their operations. I did find an interesting article about NCLB on Wikipedia, which included substantial discussions of opinions pro and con.

I left the field of special education in 1994 when I retired to Venice, Florida, although I never really left it in my thoughts and heart. But, inevitably, distancing from current events takes place.

In 1993, just prior to my retirement, I was asked to join the board of directors of the Interboro Mutual Indemnity Insurance Company, which was based on Long Island. Later that year, I had a similar invitation from the Roslyn Bank, a savings bank, and finally I received an invitation from Pall Corporation, the leader in high technology filtration and separation. Happily, I was elected to all three boards either by the other directors, policyholders or shareholders.

It was a wonderful opportunity for me to wind down from my leadership roles in the government and at NCDS. It afforded me enormous stimulation learning about the insurance and banking industries, as well as the highly intricate Pall Corporation and its worldwide production and sales. No chance of my brain retiring.

Shortly after I arrived in Venice in 1994, I began pursuing my lifetime interest in journalism, which started in high school and continued in college when I was co-editor of the *Muhlenberg Weekly*. The *Sarasota*

Herald-Tribune hired me as a correspondent to write restaurant reviews for its Monday feature on business lunches. The editors called the column "Power Lunch," which was not my first choice of titles, but they were paying the bills. I also wrote a series of brief reports about the travels Peggy and I undertook around the world by ship, stopping on all seven continents. From time to time, I would write a public policy column about local affairs in Venice and Sarasota County.

When I could not develop a regular weekly or bi-weekly schedule with the Herald-Tribune, I approached the Venice Gondolier Sun, then a three-times-a-week publication with a direct focus on Venice. I soon found myself taking on the "establishment" in Venice, dominated at that time by developers and their attorneys. The attorneys had developed a PAC, which had no organized opposition, and which successfully supported each city council member elected between 2000 and 2007. I wished to call my column "Tilting at Windmills," although the paper chose not to use that designation, so I just made it my email address for the column.

Some development decisions that I opposed led me to run for Mayor in 2007. It happened when two of my friends decided to run for city council. I was planning to support them in my column, but they asked me to join them in the race. Neither wanted to run for Mayor, so I did. All three of us were elected, but we did not all live happily ever after. We did make some significant changes in the land development process and the city's growth plan, and purchased or provided funds to develop four wonderful parks. But we also had to deal with small town politics which, as my wife Peggy pointed out, suggested Venice was no "Mayberry."

Along the way, I began a blog called Insideveniceflorida.com. When I was Mayor, I wrote it with some caution, and later on with more gusto and vitriol. I am pleased that at a recent count it had more than 90,000 individual hits.

***

Over the years I have been guided by a phrase from the Nobel Laureate address by the great American novelist William Faulkner. Speaking of matters of values and spirit he said, "I believe we will not only endure, we will prevail."

POSTLUDE

Much has happened since I left government service and the Department of Education in 1981, much of it positive. Millions of children have received special education services. Appropriations have come a long way since the $2.5 million in 1967, the first year of the Education of the Handicapped Act, and the $300 million when PL 94-142 began. For fiscal year 2012, the Obama Administration requested $12.6 billion as the federal share of educating children of preschool and school age.

I recall again the conversation with Wilbur Cohen, former Secretary of HEW and a major architect of Medicare, who asked me during the development of S. 6 and H.R. 70, "How much money will it take to achieve what you want?" I remember dreaming big and replying, "It will not meet the needs, but if we can grow to $1 billion, I think we can change the system forever." Considering we received about $50 million in federal funds at that time, that was dreaming big indeed.

Most significantly, the United States no longer accepts excluding children with disabilities from school programs. What was once commonplace practice is now unthinkable.

Major Trends

The language in PL 94-142 called for children with disabilities to be educated with non-handicapped children when appropriate. This was the key concept in the provision of "free, appropriate, public education." Since then, a major shift in educational thought and practice has taken place, which has been given the name "inclusion."

It began with the efforts to end the exclusion of children, often with severe disabilities, from the schools. Many states had programs for children with severe to moderate mental retardation in state schools and programs run by other state agencies. PARC, mentioned earlier, established under a federal court consent agreement that children with mental retardation could not be excluded from public education in the State of Pennsylvania.

PL 94-142 made that provision nationwide. Among the earliest supporters of inclusion programs were the professionals working with severely handicapped children. They formed an organization, The Association for the Severely Handicapped (TASH), with some financial and technical assistance from the Bureau of Education for the Handicapped. Founded in 1975, TASH has played an active role in the development of educational programs.

Yet, today there is a significant divide between two groups who deal with disabled children. One side supports "full inclusion," which in many areas has come to mean educating all children with disabilities in regular classrooms. The other side favors the overall philosophy but is concerned that in application, inclusion provides less, rather than more, specialized instruction to children.

Inclusion has had great appeal for many parents, and the supporters testify that they have seen positive gains for children with disabilities as a result of being in close classroom contact with non-disabled children. Those of us in the field over the years have experience with separate classes including children with very different educational needs, simply for administrative purposes.

School district and state administrators have also embraced the program, but in their embrace one can see signs of appreciating it as a cheaper solution rather than a range of services under a special education model.

Some experts have told me they see a threat to special education, perhaps its dissolution, because of the over-application of inclusion. They point to states changing their specialized teacher certification systems in relation to categorizing children into just two groups, "high incidence" and "low incidence." The former describes children with learning disabilities, behavioral problems, etc., while the latter refers to children with severe disabilities. According to the experts, this leads to an inevitable diminution of the teacher's specific skills and depth of information about any one disability.

In a parallel observation, some feel that special education as a discipline is under attack from people who feel "it has not worked."

No Child Left Behind

The act known as No Child Left Behind, (NCLB), which was passed during the Bush Administration in 2001, placed an emphasis on academic testing of children and linking the results with teacher and school performance. It was welcomed by many as increasing "accountability," i.e. determining school value by children's scores. States had freedom to design standardized tests for their statewide evaluations. But the law also raised the specter of "failing schools" and reductions in funding, or even forced closure, for those educational establishments where test scores fell much below average.

In practice, this approach, while still having some supporters, has proved problematic. Testing has varied from state to state. Texas and Florida, for example, both boasted of marked increases in performance on their tests. However, on the National Assessment of Education, they remained in a lower percentile, virtually unchanged from previous results.

Recently, states have petitioned the federal Department of Education to give them waivers from the penalties, and a number have been granted. The questions about mainstreaming children with disabilities, non-English speakers, etc. that some had embraced, have also proven troublesome. When they have been included in the testing, average scores for schools have been negatively affected, leading to requests to be able to measure the children without these conditions to meet the law's criteria for success.

Federal education funding has increased dramatically under NCLB, leading to the evolution of PL 94-142 into the amended law now known as The Individuals with Disabilities Education Act (IDEA). As was easily predicted, the somewhat conflicting results have led to sharply varying views of the law's effectiveness.

Response to Intervention (RTI)

Perhaps the most interesting evolution in education in recent years has been the development of the teaching process called "Response to Intervention" (RTI).[13] The program grew out of dissatisfaction with the process used to identify children with learning disabilities for special education services. Supporters see it as an opportunity to provide educational services without having to label a child as learning disabled or otherwise disabled. Further, intervention with RTI should reduce referrals to special education as the interventions help remediate many learning problems without having to resort to such referrals.

Many detractors understand and applaud the intentions, but are concerned about the effectiveness of RTI's implementation outside of what might be called "laboratory" conditions, that is, where the teachers are well trained and observed and the requirements for research-based instruction are carefully maintained.

In PL 94-142 children with specific learning disabilities were defined using a mechanism that compared their IQ from a standardized test with their performance usually in reading, but occasionally in spelling, math, etc. This approach became known as the discrepancy model—if the reading scores were significantly lower than the IQ scores, that discrepancy indicated a learning disability. School professionals also were to make judgments of the child's performance and, through the Individual Education

---

13 Professors Doug and Lynn Fuchs, who have played major parts in this development, have published a very informative report on RTI in the article, "The Blurring of Special Education," *Exceptional Children*, Vol. 76, no. 3, pp. 301-323, Spring, 2010.

Plan, propose special education programs designed to help. This often was provided in resource room programs in which the child spent part or even a full day.

As PL 94-142 was implemented, the category "learning disabled" experienced the fastest growth in the number of children identified as needing special education. This created financial demands on the system. The discrepancy model also was questioned on a variety of bases including whether children had to fall too far behind before the discrepancy was determined. Some school districts and states felt that there should be a two-year discrepancy before a "learning disability" could be identified requiring special education. Critics felt that a child reading, for example, at a second-grade level when in grade four, was very much harmed by the designation. Others felt, conversely, that the judgment of teachers and instructional staff was too subjective, and so too many children were identified and labeled inappropriately.

The literature of the period discloses a range of articles criticizing the discrepancy model and suggesting that there really was no difference between poor or slower readers and children in special education identified as learning disabled.

Experts in learning disability today report real fears that educators might make the case that special treatment programs, e.g. special education and special teachers of children with learning disabilities, should be ended and the children "included" in the regular classroom. The fear is, and I share it, that we will return to the time before PL 94-142, when large numbers of children in regular education received no real instruction. Eventually they lost interest in school and dropped out.

RTI as an Answer to the Discrepancy Model?

The basic approach of RTI is to screen the entire group of children in a given grade or program and, using standard measures, identify those performing below a certain level to determine who is at risk for failure.

Those children become candidates for Tier One instruction in a regular program using research-based instruction for a period of time, often six weeks. At the end of that time, the children are screened again to see how they have responded to instruction. If their performance is still lacking, they are moved to Tier Two and receive more intensive instruction. (I am not going to attempt to provide a detailed description of procedures, models, etc., as there is extensive literature on the subject.) After a time period of progress monitoring, should the child still be lagging behind, the referral to Tier Three is made. That is essentially where special education and the processes under PL 94-142/IDEA begin to be applied, such as the Individual Education Plan, etc.

At present, RTI is popular in many school districts among many parents and educators. However, advocates and concerned detractors alike agree that talking about RTI and delivering it effectively are two different things. RTI depends on quality instruction using models that have been evaluated as effective. As such, it requires well trained teachers, and careful adherence to the methods and reliable testing. There is agreement among top professionals that many schools are not fulfilling these requirements. Nonetheless, there are successful programs in place and testimonials to its effectiveness are not hard to find. The question is, will "saving money" rule the day, or will careful programs, despite being somewhat more costly, become widespread?

Some years ago I remember Professor Joe Torgesen reporting on his study of the results from the application of carefully researched instruction (separate from RTI, per se). He commented that his results were positive for most children, but there was a bottom three to five percent who did not respond as well as the others. Those, he felt, represented a target population for intensive specialized, instruction. My conversations with experts in RTI disclose a similar population that will not benefit from the RTI process. Let it be said that exactly how to develop that needed instruction so that it succeeds is still a work in progress, although a promising one.

In Conclusion

Two separate, yet philosophically linked, movements have developed over the years since 1981. Each relates to the idea of educating children in the regular classroom. RTI is an attempt to be sure that what happens in that classroom is based on scientific developments and is more carefully delineated than what is often the case. In most schools a special education teacher is an adjunct to the regular teacher, perhaps offering small group instruction or, more rarely, individual instruction. The effectiveness of that instruction depends a great deal on the abilities of the teacher.

In the years since 1981, the pendulum has swung from too much separation to "inclusion" and probably too little separation. That is not a universally held opinion, however, and as I see it, there have been both good and bad examples of the efforts to include children in regular education programs.

The primary good, it seems to me, comes from a new interest in trying to assist children in special education to reach higher goals of academic and social abilities. The disadvantage is that some programs, in the name of the philosophically attractive "inclusion," have essentially moved away from a key provision of PL 94-142—developing a program based on the individual needs of each child.

When the resource room or the special class was always the place where children were referred after their evaluation, it was not really an individual education plan. When the children always are placed in regular classrooms, however, it is the opposite extreme of the same problem.

I am not ready to assume—and many of the top research workers in the field are not either—that all children have needs which can be met in the regular classroom. Special education for some children is highly specialized and labor-intensive. Where special education programs fail, it is usually because more is needed, not less. That is the situation we face today. Clearly what some have called "The Quiet Revolution," growing from PL 94-142 and its predecessors, has accomplished a great deal in increased provision of services, but the hope for instruction proven effective for children is still a work in progress—attracting optimists and pessimists about its outcome.

The breakthrough for special education between 1965 and 1981 also played a major role in changing the public perception and attitudes toward children and adults with disabilities, leading to the later passage of the Americans with Disabilities Act of 1990. This act has influenced employment, transportation, architecture and more, making profound differences in the lives of Americans with disabilities.

***

I am grateful for having had the chance to play a role in bringing about real change in the American education system and, more importantly, in the lives of children with disabilities and their families.

If the system has not solved all the problems of education, it must be lauded for its embrace of all children and its attempt to solve a problem on a scale never before attempted by other nations. In the late 1960s and 70s, I met in Copenhagen with Special Education Inspector Skov Jorgenson and colleagues from the Nordic countries. We stayed in touch during the development of PL 94-142 and its implementation. The public health and education system in Denmark presumed appropriate care for the disabled from pre-natal through geriatric stages, and so it provided excellent services. Skov told me the U.S. approach to education as an intrinsic right for all and the dedication to including children wherever appropriate with non-disabled children was a unique approach he admired very much.

In the years following the passage of PL 94-142, I was invited to discuss the "American" experience before a number of international organizations in England, Scotland, China and several Iron Curtain countries before the end of the Communist era. I found that all over the globe, people shared an interest and respect for the efforts of the United States.

The many people and organizations named in this book clearly have made a mark on history.

INDEX

Edwin W. Martin

From 1965 to 1981, Edwin Martin had a hand in every piece of legislation in Washington, D.C., that impacted children with disabilities. Working with Congress in Democratic and Republican administrations, he was an architect of the Education for All Handicapped Children Act of 1975, now known as IDEA, and served as the nation's first Assistant Secretary of Education for Special Education and Rehabilitative Services. He later was a lecturer at the Harvard Graduate School of Education, teaching public policy and special education, and an Adjunct Professor of Education at Columbia University's Teachers College, while heading the National Center for Disabilities Services in New York. He lives with his wife, Peggy, in Venice, Florida.

For more information
and to contact the author,
go to

www.breakthroughspecialed.com
and ed@breakthroughspecialed.com

www.ingramcontent.com/pod-product-compliance
Lightning Source LLC
LaVergne TN
LVHW091045080826
845145LV00002B/636

* 9 7 8 1 9 3 8 8 4 2 0 5 4 *